bir

☐☐☐☐☐

www.itchybirmingham.co.uk

© itchy Ltd
Globe Quay Globe Road Leeds LS11 5QG
t: 0113 246 0440 f: 0113 246 0550 e: all@itchymedia.co.uk
ISBN: 1-903753-13-9

City Editor	Simon Smith
Senior Contributor	Phil Vinter
Editorial Team	Philippa Black, John Emmerson Simon Gray, Gayle Hetherington, Mike Waugh, Andrew Wood
Design	Matt Wood, Chris McNamara
Contributors	Matt Alford, Naomi Cassidy, Nick Dixon, Max Kandhola, Brett Morton, Alison Swann, John Sparks, Alexa Stewart, Matt Tootell
Acknowledgements	Cathy Harrison @ Birmingham Marketing Partnership

The views expressed in this publication are those of the authors and contributors and are not necessarily those held by the editors or publishers. Readers are advised to form their own opinions and we welcome any contributions. All details, listings, addresses, phone numbers are correct to our knowledge at the time of going to print. itchy Ltd cannot be held responsible for any breach of copyright arising from the supply of artwork from advertisers.

HIRE ME
OH YES, SUBLIMINAL ADVERTISING. THE JOB'S YOURS.
BEWARE OF THE VOICES. FOR CAREER ADVICE WORTH LISTENING TO AND THOUSANDS OF JOBS. VISIT
monster.co.uk

contents

introduction + two days/hours 5

restaurants 10

bars 32

pubs 52

clubs 68

gay 80

body 83
health clubs • beauty • sun tanning • tattooists • hairdressers

shopping 86

entertainment..98
cinema • theatre • live music • comedy • sports • activities
snooker/pool • bowling • golf • casinos • galleries/museums

takeaway 114

laters 116

accommodation 118

useful info 120
travel • local media

map + index 124

top fives

Eats To Impress 16	Watch the Footy 59
Late Eating.............................25	Outdoor Drinking 65
Cheap Eats 29	Places To Pull 76
Happy Hours 36	Late Drinking 117

calling all writers

We're looking for writers for itchybirmingham.co.uk. Experts who know their stuff across every area – music, clubs, restaurants, bars, the arts – the whole shebang. Whatever your speciality, if you'd like to get involved, then send us an email to **birminghamwriters@itchymedia.co.uk** with a sample of either a venue review or something entertaining you've written, and we'll have a read through and get in touch.

birmingham 2002

'Here we are, bloody Spaghetti Junction… damn, wrong exit. Oh no, we're heading for… BIRMINGHAM!'.

To those that don't live here, Britain's second city has always been somewhere to skirt around on the way to a 'nicer' destination. The former powerhouse of the industrial revolution has, however, been enjoying a prolonged facelift since the 1980s and the Birmingham city centre of 2002 is smart, modern and pleasant to the eye. Whether it's shops, clubs, bars or food you're after, Brum can compete with the best of them.

Furthermore, the city centre will soon boast a brand new, totally revamped BullRing shopping centre and fingers crossed will be the new home for the national football stadium. So, whether you're a local trying to keep up with a city whose visage is changing quicker than Michael Jackson's, or an outsider who has been fortunate enough to take a wrong turning off the Spag, indulge in the cream and the dregs, that this ever-improving city has to offer.

itchy Birmingham 2002 has been completely rewritten and updated to make sure you've got the most bang up-to-date information available. For those new to the city, the explosion of nightlife has left a few key 'destination' areas to go out in, oddly enough all dotted around the centre and south of the city, and that's how we've divided the drinking sections of the guide.

City:
Aston Triangle: Right next to the uni, there's not a lot, but it's here nonetheless.
Broad Street: Shiny, glitzy and mostly townie, including Brindleyplace and Gas Street.
Central: Broadly covering everywhere from Millennium Square down to Digbeth and Hurst Street.
St Pauls: Hockley, part of Jewellery Quarter.

Other areas:
Harborne: Drinker's suburbia with leafy trees and plenty of boozers.
Moseley: Still the Bohemian part of Birmingham, though chain pubs are doing their best to rid the area of individuality.
Selly Oak: Home to Birmingham University, shed-loads of students and pubs catering to ever-thirsty crowds.

www.itchy**birmingham**.co.uk

Birmingham's Best Dance and R+B
Galaxy 102.2

Galaxy 102·2

www.galaxy1022.co.uk

Oh my God we're good to you...

Not only do we write funky little books but we also offer you, the discerning entertainment junkie, some pretty fine stuff on-line.

Point your browser to **www.itchycity.co.uk** and we'll not only keep you entertained with stories and reviews about what's going on in your city, we can also send you regular emails and SMS messages about the stuff you're into. So, we'll keep you informed about where the best happy hours are, when Oakenfold's next in town or where you can find a kebab at 2am. There's also a chance for you to contribute your views and reviews and get free stuff in return (we are too good to you). Have a shoofty. Go on.

Go to www.itchybirmingham.co.uk, click on itchyme, and sign up for:

Cheap Drinks / offers • Cheap Eats / offers • House & Garage • Techno & Electronica • Jazz, Soul, Reggae & Funk • Indie • Metal & Alternative • Hip Hop, R'n'B & Breaks • Drum n' Bass & Jungle • Sixties, Northern Soul & Motown • Seventies, Eighties & Disco • Pop & Rock • Classical & Opera • World, Folk and Latin • Gay • Comedy • Stage • Art • And all the venues we feature in the book

---

itchy box set

Oh, imagine. **All 16 titles**, an encyclopaedia of entertainment across the country, all wrapped up in a glorious multi-coloured special box. Every title below in one mother of a box. Limited edition, naturally, and so exclusive, we don't even know what it looks like ourselves.

Artist's impression. Is this what the box will look like?

If you were to buy these individually, it'd cost you a bargainous £44. But hello, what's this? We're doing the full caboodle **for a mere £35**, including free postage and packing. **Call 0113 246 0440** and order by credit/debit card and we'll whizz one over to you.

bath birmingham brighton bristol cambridge cardiff edinburgh glasgow leeds liverpool london manchester nottingham oxford sheffield york

Two Hours in Birmingham

You've probably arrived at New Street Station, and with so much building and renovation work, you'd be forgiven for thinking that Brum's a dump. Before you write it off, you've still got a few options:

i) Hurst Street/Arcadian Centre: Housing the more individual and salubrious bars in the city. Go out past the taxi ranks on the ground floor of New Street, turn right and take your first left.

ii) Mailbox: As above, but instead of taking your first left, keep going, and when you get to the huge roundabout, you can't miss it. Massive swanky shopping/bar/restaurant complex for those with a few quid to burn.

iii) High Street Shopping: Go up the escalators from New Street into the Pallasades. And voila, there's the shops. But if you're looking for a bit more variety, come out the other side, down the ramp into New Street and take a good look around.

iv) Broad Street/Brindleyplace: Especially if it's summer, relaxing by the canal can't be beaten. As above, but turn left out into New Street and keep going, through the square, past the **Floozy in the Jacuzzi**, past the library, through **Paradise Forum** and out the other side. When you've reached a Communist-looking statue (**Going Forward**), then you're onto Broad Street. Down a lorry-load of pints (pubs), sip on a G&T (bars) or umm and ahh at the artwork (galleries) – whatever makes you happy. Turn right when you see the canal for Brindleyplace to chill by the water. Sorted. And that's about all you'll get sorted in two hours. Why the hell aren't you staying longer?

Two Days in Birmingham

The ultimate weekender

Stay – *At The Burlington Hotel*. Rooms start from around £70 and are well worth it in this stylish and centrally located hotel.

Shop – The city centre has all the usual high street stuff you'd expect and a whole lot more, but if you're feeling really flush then head to the designer label haven that is *The Mailbox*.

Attractions – *Millennium Point* looks promising, and will be open by the time you read this for the *IMAX* or *Thinktank*. Failing that, you could take a trip to **Cadbury World** in Bourneville, though as it's a Quaker area, you'll find it devoid of anything else that could be deemed as fun. *Sealife Centre* is worth a shot, or failing that you can check out the cinemas/bowling alleys in a variety of places. See entertainment.

Eat – If you're going for a blow out then I'd recommend *Le Petit Blanc*. As long as you've got the readdies then you'll be treated like royalty and can really make a night of it. Of course it would be criminal to come to Brum and not sample the local cuisine: Indian. And the **Maharajah** is as good as you'll get.

Drink – There's plenty of options. Either make a night of it 'round the **Arcadian Centre**, making sure to get a round or two at **52 Degrees North** and **Sobar**, or head up to **Broad Street** and **Brindleyplace** and check out **Ipanema** or **Casa**.

Club – Depends what you're after, naturally. Dance-wise, the new **Hidden** looks like taking over top of the bill, whereas indie kids, grungers, and those who resolutely refuse to bow to dress codes would do better moshing at the **Academy**. Rhythm, blues and jazz are well catered for at **Ronnie Scotts** or **The Jam House**.

Birmingham on the cheap

A bargainous weekend in Brum for less than £100.

Stay – There's plenty of cheap places to stay around the city, and somewhere basic like the **Ibis** in the heart of Chinatown will hardly break the bank. (£35)

Shop – **Cult Clothing** is pretty cool without being pricey, but the real bargains can be found at **A1** or **Yo Yo**. (£18, a bit random, we know)

Attractions – Well, it's got to be free really hasn't it? A few of the galleries don't charge admission, or ask for voluntary donations (don't take the piss), or you could head out to the **Lickey Hills** for some glorious countryside. Call the travel hotline for the best ways to get there. (£0)

Eat – It just has to be a balti. There's literally thousands throughout the city, and the best ones can be found in the **Balti Triangle**, and many will let you bring your own booze. See restaurant section for more. (£14)

Drink – **The Square Peg** and **The Figure of Eight** are perennial favourites with tight-wads, but if you shop around for happy hours you can get bargains at loads of places including **Bar Med** or **Bar Coast**. (£30)

Club – With all the late bars in Birmingham you can stay out 'til way past bedtime without even paying to get into a club. (£0)

Total Cost – £97.
Enough left for breakfast at Mr Egg.

www.itchy**birmingham**.co.uk

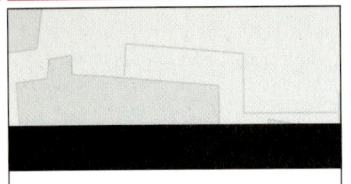

restaurants

www.itchybirmingham.co.uk

We've worked out the price of a meal for two as the cost of two main courses (in brackets), plus a bottle of the cheapest and in some cases, nastiest house white. This means it's really a bare minimum, as it doesn't include the tip, the 2nd and 3rd bottles and the inevitable but unnecessary triple whiskies and cigars at the end of the meal.

■■ The Americas

■■ T.G.I Fridays
180 Hagley Road, Edgbaston
(0121) 454 1930
Do you think there's an English-themed franchise restaurant in Austin Texas where all the waiting staff dress in morning suits, talk with received annunciation, and tell tall tales about young master Teddy and the gooseberry bush? Sounds stupid, but not as stupid as the waiters dressed like clowns hi-fiving you to a coronary hell in this long-standing OTT American-themed fries and burger joint. Portions and enthusiasm are as big as they get, and if you're into your chain restaurants, this one is actually pretty decent.
Meal for two: £37 (Fillet mignon)
Mon-Sat 12-11.30. Sun 12-11

■■ Ipanema
60 Broad Street (0121) 643 5577
When it first opened, no-one was quite sure how it'd work. Would it be a bar that'd serve up duff loosely Brazilian-themed tripe? Or an exquisite restaurant with a crappy bar tacked onto the front? Well, as Ronnie Biggs is my ageing witness, they've succeeded in both, in what's now one of the classiest

places along Broad Street. Food is on the excellent side of tasty, and because the bar and restaurant are separate, there's no chance of someone salsa-ing into you when you're trying to enjoy your jerk chicken. Recommended.
Meal for two: £34 (Red snapper)
Mon-Thu 12-11, Fri/Sat 12-11.30, Sun 12-10.30

■ ■ Las Iguanas
The Arcadian Centre (0121) 622 4466
The strongest evidence yet that there's more to Mexico than just silly hats, droopy moustaches and feisty natives that are all too eager for a knife fight. With plates of food the size of sombreros and bouncy latino music to chew along to, you can't go far wrong if you decide to bring you and your amigos here for a bit of nosh. If the tequila puts you in the mood, there's also room to shake that J-Lo collegen-injected ass, although most seem content to sit back and enjoy the atmosphere. At around £12 for a main course you'll be more than satisfied by the end of the night.
Meal for two: £31 (Brazillian lime chicken)
Mon-Fri 12-3, 6-11.30. Sat 12-11.30.
Sun 12-10.30

■ ■ Nando's
Broad Street, Five Ways (0121) 616 1844
Specialising in chicken, in the loosest possible sense, like McDonald's specialise in cow. Chicken in a bun, chicken in a pitta, roast chicken, chicken on toast, with complimentary hotter than the inside of the sun Piri Piri sauces, to mask the rather minging taste. Not a restaurant as such, because you've got to lay your own table, which leaves the dour-faced waitresses little to do but snarl at you when you order. Nando's? Dildos more like.
Meal for two: £19 (Half chicken)
Mon-Sun 12-11.30

■ ■ Old Orleans
80 Broad Street (0121) 633 0144
Old, ancient and dated Orleans. These Deep-South diners started popping up in the mid-eighties and spread across the country like small pox, and are about as much fun. The food's your basic ribs and fries fare, that can be tasty if done right, which it isn't. If you've been on the piss around Broad Street all afternoon then it'll fill a gap, but I wouldn't go out of your way to come here.
Meal for two: £19.50 (Burger and fries)
Mon-Sat 12-11, Sun 12-10.30

www.itchybirmingham.co.uk

restaurants

■■ Santa Fe
178-180 Wharfside Street, The Mailbox
(0121) 632 1250

There can't be many better places to eat out on a warm summer's evening than this. Sipping one of the gorgeous strawberry daiquiris as the sun sets over the rustic Birmingham canalway, is the perfect way to relax after a hard day's work or shopping. The food served up is a combination of Native American, Colonial Spanish, and Pioneer Settler influences that form the unique culture of the city of Santa Fe in New Mexico. The fortunate consequences of this interaction is a menu that is flavoursome and varied. It's worth noting that the spicy menu provides plenty of options for vegetarians as well as hearty dishes for meat lovers. If the crisp winter air draws you inside, you won't be disappointed as it's smart, spacious and complete with an extremely well-stocked cocktail bar. Although it's not the cheapest restaurant in town, Santa Fe has an awful lot to offer, and if you're thinking of heading there towards the end of the week, it's a good idea to book in advance.

Meal for two: £29 (Chargrilled Galisteo chicken)
Food Mon-Sat 12-10.30. Sun 12-10.30.

■■ Caribbean

■■ Xaymaca Experience
34 Bristol Street (0121) 622 3332

To my knowledge this is the only Caribbean restaurant in the city, and I can't imagine too many people queuing up to go into competition with them. No, not because it's run by Yardies, but because they're damn good and would take some beating. It's a pretty small restaurant and the décor, complete with wall covering beach murals, verges on the tacky side, but it's infinitely preferable to the sort of ultra-sanitised theme restaurants that the big breweries come up with. The slightly rickety beach café style is combined with some of the most genuine, friendly service in the city. The food is spectacular, with a menu full of fruity flavours and colourful sounding dishes, all of which taste significantly better with some Caribbean bottled beers or the lethal rum punch. Eezee now.

Meal for two: £24 (Curried goat)
Tue-Sat 7-1am

■■ Chinese

■■ Cathay
Cathay Building, 86 Holloway Head
(0121) 666 7788

Slightly out of the town centre, this modern and bright Chinese restaurant is worth making the effort to track down, especially if you're looking for an extensive menu of vegetarian dishes. They do have a quality selection of traditional beef, chicken, king prawn and duck dishes, but there's also a specialised menu of 'So' vegetarian dishes. And no this 'So' moniker isn't an Americanised

restaurants

way of emphasising a dish's vegetarian credentials; it's actually the soya based meat substitute that is formed into frighteningly convincing strips of beef and chicken etc.
Meal for two: £24 (Fried beef)
Mon-Sat 12-2, 5.30-11 (11.30 Fri and Sat)
Sun 12-9

■ ■ China Court Restaurant
24 Ladywell Walk (0121) 666 7031
There's so many Chinese restaurants around Chinatown (yes, really), that you'd be forgiven for thinking they might all be much of a muchness. Well, let's set the record straight – this is nearly – very nearly – the best. Everything is impressive, from the style and scale of the place through to the menus. The authentic food makes it one of the most popular joints in the area, and were it not for the occasionally (really, only occasionally) off-ish service, it'd be our number one.
Meal for two: £29.50 (King prawn with green peppers)
Mon-Sat 12-11.30. Sun 12-10.30

■ ■ Chung Ying
16-18 Wrottesley Street (0121) 622 5669
What's been niggling your chopsticks? Who's soured your pork? Who stir-fried you into a strop today? Indeed, the staff are moody as you like, but you're going to have to live with it, as the food is absolutely top draw. With over 300 dishes on the menu, true, I haven't tried them all, but having worked my way through it, I haven't hit anything that didn't taste bang-on so far. It's been here for nigh on 20 years, and no doubt will be here for twenty more, so it's no big secret – impressive, traditional decor and a slight leaning to seafood in the menu.
Meal for two: £27 (Squid with ginger)
Mon-Sat 12pm-12am. Sun 12-11

■ ■ Chung Ying Garden
17 Thorpe Street (0121) 666 6622
And, drum roll please, introducing the best Chinese restaurant in Birmingham. Not only is the food as good as any Chinese restaurant in town it also has an unmatchable friendly family atmosphere. It may be something of a cliché, but the number of Chinese customers a Chinese restaurant attracts really is a good indication of its quality and this place scores particularly highly in that respect. Whatever you order and whenever

www.itchybirmingham.co.uk

restaurants

you dine you're not likely to be disappointed, but I'd really recommend getting in for lunch and sampling the dim sum and excellent Chinese tea. The Sunday buffet is also not to be missed. The restaurant has also been recently renovated and now looks as good as it tastes.
Meal for two: £29 (Baby octopus in garlic)
Mon-Sat 12-12, Sun 12-11

■■ Simply Chinese
42 Summer Hill Road (0121) 236 3188

Mmm, I wonder what these boys do? Specialising in buffet style dining this new Cantonese restaurant does a decent line in all you can eat buffet. It's reasonably kitted out, the food's not bad and very good value, but it's not the place to go to sample the finest Chinese cooking in the city. If you're in a group or a hurry, and you don't want to spunk a load of cash, then give it a whirl, but don't expect miracles.
Meal for two: £21 (Beef with oyster sauce)
Mon-Sat 12-2, 6-11

■■ Tin Tins
The Waters Edge, Brindleyplace
(0121) 633 0888

This Cantonese restaurant could be described as the perfect convergence of eastern and western styles. But then we'd be forgetting to tell you about the off-puttingly big, bright and hotel reception-like room it's housed in. Still, it's not all bad news, as the excellent food and friendly service more than makes up for any problems you might have with the décor. Head into Chinatown and you could probably get similar quality for a little less cash – but it still represents decent value.
Meal for two: £31 (Drunken chicken)
Mon-Sat 12-11, Sun 12-10.30

■■ Wing Wah
278 Thimble Lane, Nechells
(0121) 327 7879

Surely the Chinese equivalent of a greasy spoon (greasy chopstick perhaps?) Proper Chinese food served in a stripped down basic fast-food style environment. If you want grand oriental splendour head to Chinatown, but if you just want some authentic food you won't be disappointed. There isn't the friendly family atmosphere that you get at somewhere like the ChunYing Garden and it's a pretty subdued experience, so it's best to enjoy the food and keep yourself to yourself, unless you're looking for big trouble in little China.
Meal for two: £31 (Buffet)
Mon-Sun 11-11

LOOK AT HIM, POMPOUS IDIOT.

■■ English

■■ All Bar One
Brindleyplace (0121) 644 5861

Oh I've come over all tired. I feel like snoozing. Sleeping. A big deep slumber. Sorry, what's that? Oh, yeah, All Bar One, yeah yeah, decent value food... chain pub... not bad... goodnight.
Meal for two: £25.50 (Lamb steak with basil mash)
Mon-Sun 12-11

■■ Bar Coast
The Arcadian Centre (0121) 666 4931

OK, it's hardly a restaurant but it's got to be mentioned for the breakfasts alone. They're a Sunday institution, and the only way to really recover from a heavy Saturday night to prepare for the inevitable Sunday session; and the equally inevitable mysterious bout of leprosy that'll keep you from work on Monday, but will dramatically disappear by Tuesday.
Full English breakfast £4.50
Food served 11-7

■■ Bennett's
8 Bennett's Hill (0121) 643 9293

Like an upmarket department store café, though only because it's always full of carrier-laden families examining their newly purchased smalls over an afternoon café latte. I was always taught to be wary of places that let you put your undies on the table, but it's not like one of *those* bars. Ahem. For easy access to seating, simply loudly exclaim about the one-day Rackham's Sale that's just started, honest, you'll set a stampede of shoppers rushing for the exit. The food isn't going to win any Michelin stars, but it certainly fills the gap and the batteries too. Considering that it can get quite lively in the evening, it's surprisingly relaxed during the day (and there's usually plenty of space to spread your bags over).
Meal for two: £19 (Chicken wrap)
Mon-Sat 11-11. Sun 12-10.30

■■ Bucklemaker
30 Mary Ann Street, St Paul's Square (0121) 200 2515

Being bang in the centre of Brum's financial quarter, you can expect suits talking about busting gonads or golfing handicaps in this wine bar restaurant. Which makes it sound totally crud, but give it a chance – it's actually a much friendlier and more laid-back dining experience than you might assume, especially in the evenings once the pinstripe and braces boys have gone home to mummy and daddy. The staff are all particularly helpful and more than willing to guide

TOO BUSY DIGESTING HIS FOUR HOURS LUNCH TO LISTEN TO YOU

www.itchy**birmingham**.co.uk

restaurants

novices around the extremely extensive wine lists. They do a selection of tapas, which are quite good, but my advice is to go for the traditional meals. The English dishes, like the steaks, are the specialities of the house and if you want to be impressed then you really should try it.

Meal for two: £29 (Roast beef)
Mon-Fri 12-2.30, 5.30-10.30. Sat 7-10.30

■■ Leftbank
79 Broad Street (0121) 643 4464

I asked Jeeves to bring me my finest threads, for tonight I would dine like the king that I am. A venue that oozes wealth and sophistication. A venue where praise the Lord, the clientele is made up purely of my business chums and is blessedly free of the tykes and under 25s that make up Broad Street. A venue such as Leftbank. Well, I say, what a fine evening. I wondered if the food would really be as exquisite as I had prayed, and good gracious me, my doubts were quashed when a splendid supreme of salmon was served in a rich butter sauce, accompanied by a fine crisp white wine. The chocolate fondant with white chocolate sorbet was equally delicious, leaving my taste buds delirious. Yah, yah, £24.50 a head, whatever, but the service is as magnifique as the food. And by jimminy, the interior decoration only gives us minimal clues to its former state as a bank and is pleasant enough to spend the evening there. OK, to be fair, this place isn't really snobbish at all. I'm just an oik, and I've never seen anything this fancy before.

Meal for two: £36 (2-course set menu)

Beth, 22, Physiotherapist

Best place for a relaxing drink?
Casa's a cool place
And to exercise your dancing feet?
Medicine Bar's got the right atmosphere
What about some healthy eating?
Las Iguanas. Not necessarily healthy, but...
Favourite shop? Jigsaw
What's Birmingham strongest point?
The balti houses all over the place
And its Achilles heel?
The traffic

WELL, DIGEST THIS!

16   itchy**birmingham** 2002

restaurants

■■ St Paul's
St Paul's Square (0121) 605 1001
This small and stylish restaurant specialises in a modern take on classic English dishes. The food is almost always of a high standard and decent value, and the wine list is very good. So it's above criticism then? Well if there is anything that might leave a bad taste in the mouth it's the air of superiority of the staff and the trendy crowd of 'wannabes' that you can find in there from time to time. Personally I'm baffled at how waiters on minimum wage can be arrogant about anything, or indeed why wankers would want to advertise that they are, but they do, and both nauseating types co-habit happily here in a bizarre form of arsehole heaven. Nonetheless don't let this stop you from enjoying what is very good food.
Meal for two: £25 (Bacon wrapped chicken with mustard sauce)
Mon-Sat 12-2.30, 6-10. Sun 12-6

top 5 for...
Eats to impress
1. Le Petit Blanc
2. Bucklemaker
3. The Bank
4. Shimla Pinks
5. Quod

■■ Wine Republic
Centenary Square, Broad Street (0121) 644 6464
The Republic of Wine is surrounded by the Red sea – a huge blissful ocean of deliciously potent French claret. Passing sailors often fell into this alcoholic aquatic wonder, and although their colleagues rushed to save them, they fought them off bravely. Sadly this vino paradise doesn't exist outside my deluded head, whereas this laidback bar/restaurant is attached to the Birmingham Repertory Theatre. If you're looking for a bit more culture from the menu and clientele than most places around Broad Street, then this is the place for you. It does have a strong bar-like feel, but you're not going to be deafened by dance music over your dinner. Grab a seat by their huge windows and you'll find your thoughts drifting back to the sea of slosh. "Ah, beautiful yet barbarous – my one true love".
Meal for two: £32 (2 course dinner £11.95 – salt crusted snapper.)
Food served Mon-Sun 11-2, 5-9.30

BEWARE OF THE VOICES. FOR CAREER ADVICE WORTH LISTENING TO, INCLUDING HELP WITH INTERVIEWS. VISIT monster.co.uk

www.itchybirmingham.co.uk

restaurants

■■ European

■■ 52 Degrees North
The Arcadian Centre, Hurst Street
(0121) 622 5250

An undisputed leader in the bar scene, 52 Degrees divides opinion as a dining experience. With a definite in-crowd, it might seem a bit alienating for some, but if you want to see and be seen, then this is the place. The food is extremely good, fusing elements from European and Asian cooking, and the place is very stylish, but many people would hope for a bit more intimacy if they're spending this kind of money. Fortunately most of the girls in here don't eat much anyway.
Meal for two: £46 (based on a 2-course meal)
Mon-Wed 5-11, though bar's open 'til later Also see bar section.

■■ Casa
Brindleyplace (0121) 633 3049

This is the best bar/restaurant in Brindleyplace and could hold its own in any location in town. In the evening it's definitely a bar, and a damn good one at that, but earlier on and through the day it's an excellent place to eat. Whether you go for one of the simply presented sandwiches or one of the more exotic dishes from the small but appetising menu, you won't be disappointed by the quality. Only the most miserly will be disappointed by the prices, considering that many of the main dishes are only a couple of quid more than you'd pay at most fast food places. They do a selection of tapas and meze starters too, which are great if you're just after a snack, or if you only really came in for a drink but are feeling tempted.
Meal for two: £25 (Grilled fillet of Queenfish). Mon-Sun 11-11

■■ Denial
120-122 Wharfside Street, The Mailbox
(0121) 643 3080

"I haven't split up with my girlfriend, we're just having a break. She needs a little space at the moment, some time to find herself. We'll be back together in time for Christmas." That's right, I'm in denial. Crap jokes aside, if you're looking for some top-

18　　　　　　　　　　　　　　　itchy**birmingham** 2002

drawer world cuisine then you should be in Denial too. This stylish newcomer to the scene is rapidly gathering a loyal following, as much for drinking as dining. Thankfully the eating area is away from the casual lounging area by the bar. "Did you hear about King Tut's yacht? It's in de Nile too!" It all becomes clear why Kathy left me.
Meal for two: £42 (Maple glazed duck)
Breakfast served: 8-10, Brunch: 10-6, Dinner 6-11
Also see bar section.

The Green Room
Hurst Street (0121) 605 4343
Perhaps seen by some as more of a café bar, the Green Room certainly warrants a mention for excellent food, as well as the fine coffee. Very friendly and more relaxed than many places around Hurst Street and the Arcadian Centre.
Also see bar section.
Meal for two: £27.50 (Chicken and tiger prawn béarnaise)
Food served Mon-Thu 12-10.30. Fri-Sat 12-1.15. Sun 12-11.30

French

Bank
4 Brindleyplace (0121) 633 7001
A revolutionary addition to Birmingham's eateries when it opened, and to some extent it still is. Ultra-modern, stylish, cosmopolitan on one hand, and expensive, lively, loud and abrupt service on the other. Without a trout it's made a big impression though, and opinion's still divided on whether or not it's a swanky London-esque addition to the restaurant scene or an over-priced style over substance place. The food is pretty special, the service is pretty hurried, and the name is pretty lame. Make up your own minds.
Meal for two: £41 (Chargrilled chicken with creamed polenta)
Mon-Sat 12-3, 5.30-11. Sun 11-10

Berlioz Restaurant
Burlington Hotel, 6 Burlington Arcade, New Street (0121) 633 1737
The standards set by the hotel, which has to be the best in town, are carried through here in this supreme French restaurant. There's been a dramatic improvement in city centre options in recent years, with the Bank and Petit Blanc raising the standards, but Berlioz can still cut it with the new kids on the block. Luxurious surroundings and fantastic cuisine, what more could you ask for? Well, a bit more change out of fifty quid wouldn't go amiss, but that's not going to happen is it?
Meal for two: £40.45 (Honey & ginger duck)
Mon-Sat 12-2.30 6.30-10, Sun 6.30-9.30

restaurants

■■□ Bistro Lyonnaise
13 St Mary's Row, Moseley
(0121) 449 9618

Like a little piece of Burgundy transported to deepest darkest Moseley this highly authentic French bistro may be little more than a pokey smokey room but it serves some of the most convincingly French cuisine in Birmingham. It's even had le thumbs up from French friends of mine who've been more than impressed by the generously portioned and well-crafted food on offer.

Meal for two: £30 (Pie Français)
Mon-Sun 12-2, 7-11

■■□ Café Rouge
Bindley Place (0121) 643 6556

These places are so variable. It's not the food so much, (it all tastes batch cooked anyway) but the ambience and feel. If you can imagine trying to have a romantic dinner on the Holte End then you get the idea of how cramped and busy this place gets. The staff seem permanently stressed and hurried, like they can't wait to see the back of you. Suits me fine, as this place is overpriced and overrated. It's pleasant enough in the summer but not enough to justify how mystifyingly popular it gets.

Meal for two: £34.50 (Roast duck with red cabbage)
Mon-Sat 10am-11. Sun 12-10.30

■■□ Le Petit Blanc
9 Brindleyplace (0121) 633 7333

My advice for this place is to go the whole hog. Make the effort, get your glad rags on, work up a hunger (and a thirst) and enjoy yourself. It's quite a different experience to The Bank but both restaurants are united by their modern cosmopolitan approach, and are completely refreshing venues in their own right. Le Petit Blanc is quite large, light, airy and modern, providing a perfect environment for socialising as well as dining. The food's always very good and the atmosphere is second to none. It's not cheap, but nor does it induce the sort of wallet raping, where you'd have to become a merchant banker to afford it – which is a relief. If you are a merchant banker... bad luck.

Meal for two: £34 (Fillet steak)
Mon-Sat 11-11.30. Sun 11-10.30

BIRMINGHAM'S BEST DANCE AND R&B

Galaxy 1022
www.galaxy1022.co.uk

■■ Indian and Pakistani

The national dish is now Chicken Tikka Masala, and with Birmingham being home to the balti, by our quick calculations, Brum should be the capital of the country. Still, until then, tuck into the finest that this city has to offer, with a whole host of balti houses in Sparkbrook. Stratford Rd, Ladypool Rd and Stoney Lane form the infamous Balti Triangle, where you can get lost for hours in Asian food.

■■ Adil's Balti
148-150 Stoney Lane (0121) 449 0335
This Balti house has been around for donkeys, which is exactly what the lamb Madras tastes…Oh bollocks. I've been dying to use that joke, but it's simply not true. This might be a dingy basic backroom of a balti house but the food is unknockable at these prices. I should have saved the gag for the Khanum later on. Can we pretend you didn't read it here? No? Sod you then.
Meal for two: £13 (Lamb bhuna, no wine)
Mon-Sun 12-12

■■ Café Lazeez
116 Wharfeside Street, The Mailbox
(0121) 643 7979
Flock wall paper, ceramic elephants, and Indian tapestries just wouldn't look right in the ultra clean surrounds of the Mailbox and thankfully you won't find any of that here in this modern and fresh restaurant. In keeping with the name, this place does have something of a café feel, but not your typical plastic tabled greasy spoon, more your modern continental café bar type. A typical balti house regular might also be taken aback by the modern approach taken to pricing as well. With most main courses beginning at around the eight pound mark, it might be a bit more expensive than your Sparkbrook favourite, but considering the location and the quality of the food you should appreciate that it's about a fair price.
Meal for two: £33 (Leg of lamb with green herbs)
Mon-Sat 11-11. Sun 11-10.30

■■ Celebrity Balti
44 Broad Street (0121) 643 8969
Named after the legendary dish that Madhur Jaffrey concocted in 20 minutes out of nothing but some marge, olive oil and gravel in a very lively episode of Ready Steady Cook. The chef then went on to host chat shows, appear in sitcoms, and promote charity fun

The Daily Telegraph — Britain's biggest-selling quality daily newspaper

www.itchybirmingham.co.uk

restaurants

runs. He finally fell from grace with the BBC when he failed to curry favour with British diners. Not believing me? Well whatever it takes to be a celebrity, the food in here is a legend in its own lunchtime. Most of the really good Indian restaurants in town are rather more traditional than the Balti style cooking here, but the food is as good as any of its rivals. Quite unique amongst Indian restaurants, this is neither the old school low-lit seventies throwback or the new school modernly minimalist Indian restaurant. It does in fact look like a pub.

Meal for two: £21 (Vegetable balti)

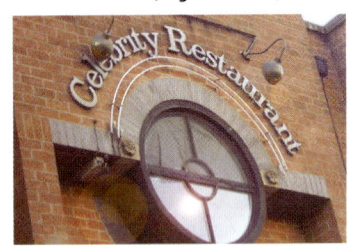

they're also excellent value and the staff are really friendly. If you're going to be addicted to something in Moseley, this is probably your safest bet.

Mon-Thur 6-1am, Fri-Sat 6-2am, Sun 6-12

I was the King of Balti's
230-232 Ladypool Road, Sparkbrook
A memorial...

"I am King of Balti's" was known across the city – you had to admire their cheek even if you didn't admire their chicken tikka. You'd be pretty unlikely to find a truly bad curry 'round these parts and 'the King' was part of the crown. True, true, the food was pretty average, and the only real King of the Balti's here was the bloke outside with a curry dish on his head and a can of Special Brew, and he thought this place was great, but then again he was mad, poor bugger. Now it's closed down, all that's left is to shed a tear, and to encourage restaurant owners everywhere to change their names in honour.

Meal for two: alas no more

Diwan
3 Alcester Rd, Moseley (0121) 442 4920

Back in the day when I was a fully-fledged card-carrying member of BA (Baltiholics Anonymous) I used to eat in Diwan about 5 nights a week. Since moving out of Moseley I've managed to keep the urges under a reasonable amount of control. It does still call me back regularly, but I'm just taking it one day at a time. So what singles Diwan out from the balti crowd? Well not only are all the dishes authentic and individual, but

Indi
The Arcadian Centre (0121) 622 4858

The bleached white brilliance of Indi would pass the Daz doorstep challenge with flying colours (although the term 'flying colours' seems somewhat inappropriate). This is truly minimalist in design with white walls, white floors, and a white bar, and if there is any artwork on the walls it must be of the Polar Bear in a snowstorm variety. Thankfully the clientele add a splash of colour and there are plans underway to introduce some more

The Daily Telegraph — Britain's biggest-selling quality daily newspaper

casual seating to encourage enhanced levels of lounging. The food is a novel combination of Indian cuisine served in a Mediterranean tapas style, and whilst that might sound a little confused it works surprisingly well.
Meal for two: Pollo makhani £4.45
Open late 'til 12am Mon-Wed, 1am Thu, 2am Fri-Sat
Happy hour: 12-8 house wine 2 for 1

■ ■ Jewel in the Crown
125 Alcester Road (0121) 449 4335
A complement that's often said of curry houses is that 'it's so good you should eat there sober'. Ignore this advice in here, ensure you're titted, twatted or have had a huge shot of mescaline before attempting to dine here, and you'll fit in with the majority of the other punters. Saying that, the food's on the tasty side of average, and the service is reassuringly polite and efficient. And, if you don't remember mooning at the chefs through the window at the end of the restaurant from your last visit, they'll grinningly remind you. Guaranteed.
Meal for two: £17.50 (Chicken korai)
Mon-Thur 6-12am, Fri-Sat 6-1am

■ ■ J Jay's
2 Edgbaston Shopping Centre (0121) 455 6871
This is really your archetypal Indian restaurant, very traditional and quite reserved it's the kind of place you'll find anywhere in the country. No-one could talk me into believing this is the best Indian in Birmingham, but the food is very good, and it makes for a pleasant, if slightly reserved night.
Meal for two: £23.50 (Chicken with coconut)
Mon-Fri 12-2.30, 6-12. Sat-Sun 6-12

■ ■ K2
Alcester Road, Moseley (0121) 449 3883
An upmarket alternative to most Moseley Indians this Kashmiri restaurant is a classy affair. In complete contravention to the old laws of Indian catering, this place is not only modern and stylish, it has also dispensed with the piped sitar music so fondly used in balti houses in favour of a blues and jazz soundtrack. This sets the tone perfectly and creates an excellent ambience, which is equalled by the fantastic food. There is so much to recommend that it's hard to single out individual dishes but the meat koshtavi; the kashmiri kwan; the curried fish and the garlic chicken are all spot on. It's more expensive than your average run of the mill curry house but it's quite simply better as

www.itchybirmingham.co.uk

restaurants

well. If you're not fussy or flush then try the Jewel in the Crown next door.
Meal for two: £23 (Chicken masala)
Mon-Sun 6-11.30

■ ■ Khanum
510 Bristol Road, Selly Oak
(0121) 471 4877
Just calm down. Take a seat. I'll write this very slowly. Sorry about that. I assumed you were drunk. You'd have to be to eat here. This is proper bargain basement balti. Take the novel approach of not throwing your food around or swearing at the staff and you'll be treated like royalty. Students, naturally, love the place and come swarming in droves to eat, drink and make arses of themselves.
Meal for two: £14 (Chicken biriani) exc wine
Mon-Sat 6-11 Sun 7-10.30

■ ■ Maharaja
23/25 Hurst Street (0121) 622 2641
This is the closest thing to genuine Indian cooking you'll find in Birmingham, and probably England as well. Balti may be a purely English phenomenon (and an extremely enjoyable one at that) but this is the real deal. This authentic taste of back home is what encourages Indian visitors to the city to make a point of coming here (expect to see Sachin Tendulkar and co. in here when the Indian cricket team are in town.)
Meal for two: £29 (Chicken with spinach)
Mon-Sat 12-2, 6-11

■ ■ Rajdoot Restaurant
12-22 Albert Street (0121) 643 8805
Picture the scene. It's July. You're in the Costa Del Sol. It's 90 degrees in the shade. You know what you want, don't you? That's right. Curry. Yes this is where it all began for the Rajdoot chain that has spread as far as Fuengirola (I kid you not). This traditional yet stylish tandoori restaurant has been open for over thirty years, and picked up more than a handful of awards over time, including regular recognition from Egon Ronay. Another restaurant that's a bit pricier than your aver-

top 5 for...
Late eating
1. Xaymaca Experience (1am)
2. Chung Ying (1am)
3. King of Baltis (12ish)
4. Thai Edge (12)
5. Adil's Balti (12ish)

age balti house, but I think most people these days are starting to accept that there's so much more to Indian cooking than a chicken tikka after a night in the pub.
Meal for two: £26 (Tandoori chicken)
Mon-Sat 12-2, 6.30-11.30. Sun 6.30-11.30

Shimla Pinks
214 Broad Street (0121) 633 0366
Probably the first restaurant to drag the image of Indian cuisine out of the seventies. With the style and feel more associated with modern continental restaurants, it eschewed the old stereotypes of flock wallpaper and sitar music. This modern approach quickly made the restaurant a trendy place to be seen, with plenty of celebs popping to sample the quality food. But as the number of similarly stylish Indian restaurants has grown, around the country as well as the city, Shimla Pinks has decided to go for a complete renovation to stay ahead of the pack. Can't say how it's going to look at the moment, but I'd be surprised to see rolls of maroon velvet carpet getting shipped in.
Ring for details

Spice Exchange
1845 Pershore Road (0121) 451 1007
Impressive styling, an even more impressive menu and nearly unsurpassable quality. The menu, whilst not the largest, is one of the most varied and original with some dishes you won't find elsewhere. There's even Indian beers on tap, so I can't recommend it highly enough, other than to say it's probably as good as the Maharaja in its own way.
Meal for 2 £21(Chicken tikka masala)
Sun-Thur 6-12, Fri-Sat 6-1

Italian

Bella Pasta
102 New Street (0121) 643 1548
Statistically, at least 5% of the worst chefs in Britain must live in Birmingham, and sadly most of them have jobs in the kitchen of this piss poor pasta place. Nonetheless Bella Pasta does fill a niche if you're around Broad Street and feeling peckish, but you don't want to take any risks with your wallet or your taste buds. Reasonable if uninspiring standard décor, the food is as bog standard as most bogs, and how appetising is that?
Meal for two: £27 (Chicken with tomato)
Mon-Sat 11-11. Sun 12-10.30

Caffé Uno
126 Colmore Row (0121) 212 0599
The thing that sets Caffe Uno apart is that they always seem to have more personality and atmosphere than their chain restaurant competitors. Being lively and friendly is one thing, but it wouldn't count for much if the

restaurants

food wasn't up to scratch, which thankfully it is. They do a good line in pizza, but refreshingly for these type of places the other dishes don't represent a poor alternative.
Meal for two: £24 (Gnocchi)
Mon-Sat 10am-11. Sun 11-10.30

San Carlo
4 Temple Street (0121) 633 0251
I know some people who think this place is on the pricey side. They're wrong. Yes it's more expensive than Pizza Hut. That's because it's better. Years of conditioning from high street pizzerias have distorted our views on Italian cooking, but this is the real deal. It's also got more kerb appeal than most restaurants; it looks like people are enjoying themselves in there. Modern and light with a lively atmosphere, it gets very busy, and the staff have that certain cockiness that comes from a confidence in what they're doing. The food is top-drawer and the wine list is very good.
Meal for two: £27 (Butter fried veal)
Mon-Sat 12-11

Little Italy
**2-4 St Mary's Road, Moseley
(0121) 449 8818**
Oh bugger. Not a bad word to say about this place. Not one, not even the slightest opportunity to make some bad jokes about the service – it's personable, friendly and spot-on. No opportunity to slate the food (Italian staff know exactly what they're doing). The layout's perfect with intimate nooks for couples, tables for large groups lit by candles and a whole cosy downstairs area. And no,

---

Max, 37, Photographer

OK Max, so what's your favourite bar? Denial
Up on the latest fashions eh? And for clubbing? 52 Degrees
Quite a cool dude yeah? And for a restaurant? Chung Ying Garden
We're getting the picture. Favourite shop?
I do most of my shopping in Brighton.
Hmm. Best thing about Brum?
The Villa
Incorrect. And the worst?
The traffic

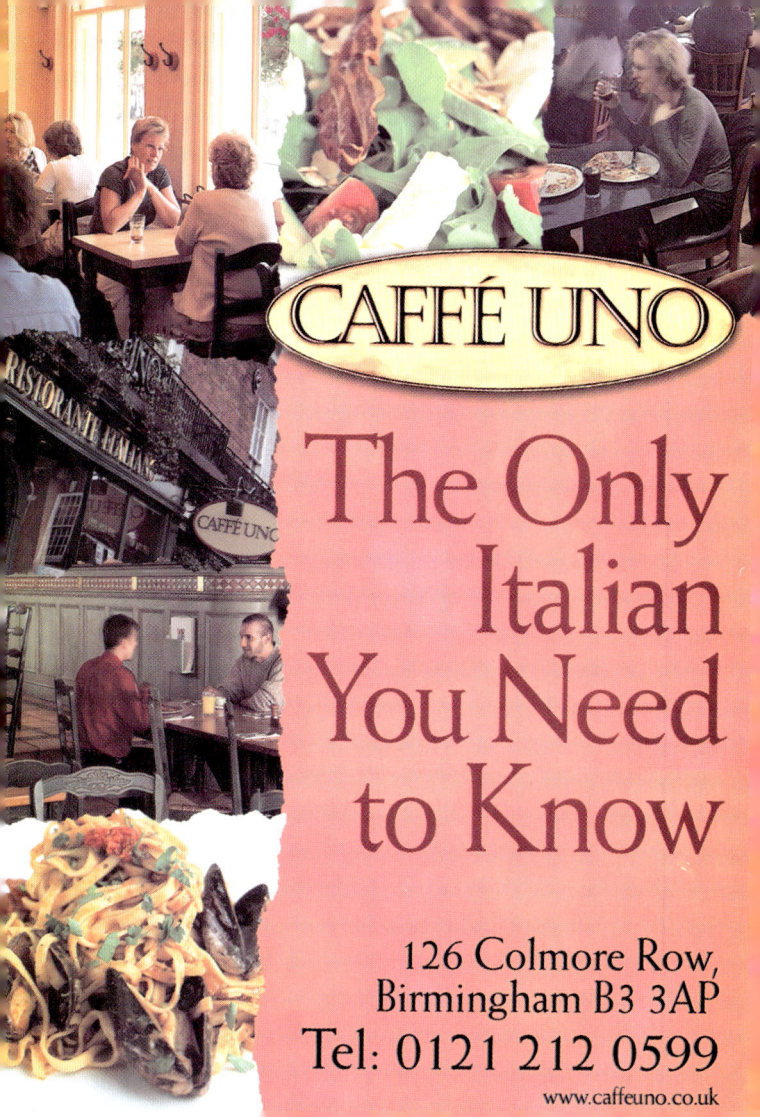

CAFFÉ UNO

The Only Italian You Need to Know

126 Colmore Row,
Birmingham B3 3AP
Tel: 0121 212 0599

www.caffeuno.co.uk

it's not in the slightest bit pretentious, with a homely feel to the whole place.
Fully recommended.
Meal for two: £16 (Cannelloni, no wine)
Mon-Sun 12–3, 5-11

■■□ Pizza Hut
Unit 202, The Arcadian Street
(0121) 643 1241
Say what you like about Pizza Hut. No really, do. As with all outlets in the chain this is a friendly family restaurant and I'm surprisingly sorry about getting barred after my indiscretion at the salad bar.
Meal for two: £25 (Stuffed-crust pepperoni)
Mon-Sat 12-11. Sun 12-10.30

■■■ Pizza Express
Brindleyplace (0121) 643 2500
Large and repetitive chain it may be, but they've still got a few things going for them. The house wine is cracking, and is such a sure fire winner that you could seduce Cliff Richard after half a bottle. This branch by the canals of Brindleyplace perhaps hasn't as much style as some other Pizza Express's, but it's always a good warm atmosphere and the food is very reliable. In fact it's fair to say that this is another quality addition to the pizza chain with that bit more style. Oh somebody shoot me.
Meal for two: £25.50 (Neptune pizza)
Mon-Sat 12-11. Sun 12-10.30

■■■ Quod
245 Broad Street (0121) 643 6744
Quod bikes. An adrenaline-thumpingly good way of reliving your racing dreams across mud tracks and farmland. Quod restaurants. A hunger-satingly good way of reliving your culinary dreams across stylish settings with modern paintings. I knew there was a connection somewhere. Sophisticated yet surprisingly good value, this mini-chain (well, there's one in Oxford anyway) pushes all the right buttons with good service, well-prepared food and a loyal number of followers.
Meal for two: £29 (Monkfish and speck salad)
Mon-Sun 11-11

■■ Zizzi
Wharfside Street, The Mailbox
(0121) 632 1333
Pitching itself as the 'new Pizza Express' this Italian chain makes you wonder what was wrong with the old one. The pizzas are at least comparable, but do we really need more of these places around the country? The place is nicely kitted out, but if you've been to a Zizzi's before you'll start to suspect that someone's scored a job lot of maroon paint at a good price. It's not strictly a pizzeria but I wouldn't stray too far from the pizzas on the menu, as there are better pasta dishes to be had elsewhere.
Meal for two: £24 (Margherita pizza)
Mon-Sat 12-11. Sun 12-10.30

■■ Japanese

■■ Shogun Teppan-Yaki
Brindleyplace (0121) 643 1856

This is the restaurant equivalent of those showboating cocktail bars, where the staff can't even serve you an orange juice without feeling compelled to throw the ice-cubes over their shoulders and back-heel them into your glass – whilst attempting a triple salko. All the food is prepared in full view, and the would be Tom Cruises take great pleasure in theatrically chopping, slicing, dicing and frying all the ingredients. Having your food prepared in such proximity does ensure freshness, but the downside is you end up smelling like you've just worked the lunchtime rush in a greasy chip shop, so be warned if you're planning on going out on the pull afterwards.

Meal for two: £25 (Vegetable tempura)
Mon-Fri 12-2.30, 6-11. Sat 6-11

top 5 for...
Cheap eats
1. Spice Exchange
2. Adil's Balti
3. Little Italy
4. Mongolian
5. Bar Coast

■■ Sobar
The Arcadian Centre, Hurst Street
(0121) 693 5084

See the bar review for more, but as far as a restaurant goes, they've done a surprisingly decent job. It's more of a boozing venue than a dining one in the evening, but you could do a lot worse than this at any time of day. Come here for the atmosphere – with an ambience changing from Pebble Mill at One (chilled and laid-back in the afternoon) to The Word (a more edgy and pre-club feel in the evenings).

Meal for two: £24 (Nasi Sobar, beef, chicken and prawns with rice)
Mon-Sat 12-12ish

■■ Teppan Yaki
Arcadian Centre, Hurst Street
(0121) 622 5183

Very similar in terms of quality to the Shogun, this restaurant doesn't have quite as much of the lively showmanship. It's still a friendly and family place but it's a bit more reserved. It comes down to a question of preference really. The food is very good but with all the flash frying there's a definite prevailing greasiness in the atmosphere, although not quite as thick as at the Shogun.

Meal for two: £28 (Fried squid and vegetables)
Mon-Fri 12-2.30, 6-11. Sat 6-11

www.itchybirmingham.co.uk

restaurants

Mongolian

The Mongolian
Ludgate Hill, St Paul's (0121) 294 2055
The thought of traditionally served Mongolian food may leave you a little nervous. Don't worry though, nobody's going to ride in on horseback and rape and pillage the kitchen staff at sword point. You simply collect a dish of raw meats and vegetable matter then hand it to the chef who cooks it right in front of you on a sizzling hot plate. Hmmm, perhaps you should still be a little nervous. Well whatever you think of the system there's no denying it tastes pretty fine, especially when washed down with a few beers. It's quite a good laugh and generates something of a party atmosphere when large groups are in, as the largely after-work crowd get into the swing of things and nobody takes it too seriously.
Open late 'til 12am all week
All you can eat £9.95

Seafood

fish!
Wharfeside Street, The Mailbox
20 Mill Lane, Touchwood, Solihull
(0121) 632 1212 (both of them)
Hello! It's fish! Happy fish! Cooked fish! Fish that are happy to be eaten! Not sure why the exclamation mark, almost as if all the staff have permanently raised eyebrows! But they don't. What they do have is a fresh and modern restaurant appropriately gazing over the canal, serving up fresh... fish! Of course, if you're a fish-fearing landlubber and the mere thought of a cod fillet brings you down with sea sickness then nothings going to convert you, not even oceanic delights of this quality. To date, the restaurants in both Leeds and London have scored top marks, and to be honest, we're pretty certain to be getting more of the same here. As if that weren't enough scaley antics they've opened another, more of the same minus the water in Solihull.
Meal for two: £31 (Monkfish)
Mon-Sat 11.30-11. Sun 12-4pm

Livebait
Broad Street
Typical. You wait ages for a seafood restaurant and then two come along at once. OK, so it was a fair few months after fish! but this similarly up-market eaterie is set to provide some excellent competition for the Mailbox restaurant. Offering the biggest selection of exotic sea creatures you'll find outside the National Sealife Centre. The whole develop-

ment of this part of Broad Street was still underway at the time of writing but the signs suggest it's going to be a classy affair.

■■ Thai

■■ Thai Edge
7 Oozells Square, Brindleyplace (0121) 643 3993

Oozells sounds like a Thai dish anyway, so it's no surprise to find Thai Mirage's sister restaurant lounging around by the canal. Like its sister, it's tasty, good-looking and willing to try anything, ranging from fiery spicey affairs to tamer encounters. Surprisingly, she charges the same as her Hurst Street sister, even though it's quite clear she's a bit more special and works on classier streets.

Meal for two: £27 (Thai green curry)
Mon-Sat 12-2.30, 6-12

■■ Thai Mirage
41-43 Hurst Street (0121) 622 2287

Smart and modern looking Thai restaurant, so much so that the proprietors opted to show the place off with full-length twelve foot windows for the front and bathed the place in white. If you've ever been tempted to take a shower or sit down for dinner in a furniture shop then now's your chance to make an exhibition of yourself. This can be off-putting at first, especially if you get a bunch of piss-head loons traipsing by on the way to PJ's, but once you're engrossed by the food you'll soon forget about it. Top quality Thai food including rich and mild dishes from the north as well as the more renowned fiery Malaysian influenced dishes.

Meal for two: £26
(Gai pad ped/stir fry chicken)
Mon-Sat 12-2.30, 6-12

---

fish! diners

fish! Diner Birmingham
156-158 Wharfside Street
Mailbox Birmingham B1 1RQ

fish! Diner Solihull
20 Mill Lane Touchwood
Solihull B91 3GS

Reservations: 0121 632 1212 On-line booking: www.fishdiner.co.uk

fish!

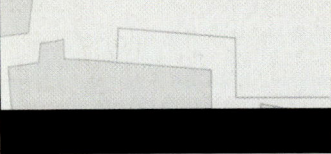

bars

www.itchybirmingham.co.uk

Bars have been exploding all over town meaning that if you can't find somewhere to suit in Brum, you're the fussiest tosser in the world, and you should really move to London. If they serve food, we've given a sample dish. And if they're open late, we've included the hours.

Arcadian Centre

With the remaining units being snapped up like the last Tracy Island toy the night before Christmas, this development is finally starting to resemble the drinking pit stop it always dreamed of becoming, when it was just a wall at the bottom of someone's garden.

52 Degrees North
The Arcadian Centre (0121) 622 5250

It was a special night in October 1983 when a convention of 52 soul lovin' sistas gathered together for one night to record a special version of 'Woman In Love' to pay homage to their favourite hot-pant wearing girl band of the 70s (The 3 degrees). They did the divas proud and in tribute to their gutsy glamour, this bar was created. Possibly. Still, 52 Degrees has the justified reputation as being one of the top bars in Brum and attracts the city's most fashionable and well turned out. The bar itself is reminiscent of an old skool cinema, complete with plush carpets and luxurious velvet curtains (not unlike the decadent wardrobes of Fayette, Sheila and Valerie themselves). Impressive, with good food and wine attracting Birmingham's beauties.

Set menu 2 courses £17 (8oz Steak)
Open late 'til 1am Mon-Wed,
2am Thu-Sat, 12am Sun.

A MELLOW MIX OF SPIRIT AND SOUL
THAT FLAVOURS WHATEVER IT TOUCHES.
MORGAN'S SPICED
FEEL THE
PRESENCE
TREVOR NELSON, DJ
Try it with soda and ice in a wild club.

bars

■■□ Arca
The Arcadian Centre (0121) 666 7777
They saved themselves a fortune whilst avoiding looking like a bunch of skinflints by going for that minimalist look apparently so favoured by the Scandinavian and Japanese nations (but really only strived for by coke-snorting traders who hate to do the dusting – gets up their noses you see). This self-styled addition to the cool collection of bars in the Arcadian Centre is awash with 'oh so tasteful' lighting... think Later with Jools Holland, rather than Good Morning Britain with Anne Diamond. There's even a courtyard, so you can pretend you're hosting your very own garden party, rather than one of your usual vomit on the doorstep shared housing affairs. Stylish and smooth.
Chicken naan £5.50
Open late 'til 2am Mon-Sat, 12.30am Sun.

■■□ Bar Coast
The Arcadian Centre (0121) 666 4931
"Bloody work-skiving tossers", muttered a Brummy builder passing by the hordes of drinkers lounging around in summer outside on the patio. Well, if you're going to skive, you could do a lot worse. One of the largest and oldest bars in the Arcadian Centre, it's as popular as ever among the mid-20s working crowd. Colourful, modern with leather couches, it strikes the precarious balance between la-di-dah 52 degrees and the pubness of O'Neill's, which all in all, means we give it the thumbs up for a visit, and the Vs to the builders.
Five spice chicken wraps £3.75
Happy hour 5-8pm 2 for 1 selected drinks.

■■□ The Green Room
Hurst Street (0121) 605 4343

I'll concede that there's definitely a room... yup, there's a door and walls and the final touch of a roof. But as yet I haven't seen even the briefest lick of olive, emerald or even khaki in here, and not a daytime talk show guest waiting to be filmed in sight. I won't be harassing Trading Standards quite yet though, as I realise there are more important aspects to a drinking hole than total title honesty. Laidback and attitude free, this bar has been here for a number of years and is slowly and steadily growing in size. Regulars might not have noticed the subtle increase, but those who only visit sporadically, like aunties at Christmas, could be forgiven for

itchy**birmingham** 2002

'Ooh! Haven't you grown' type platitudes. The Green Room also offers excellent food without any of the pretension of some of the nearby bars.
Hot spicy chicken £7.50
Open late 'til 12am Mon-Thu, 2am Fri-Sat and 12.30 Sun.

Indi
The Arcadian Centre (0121) 622 4858
See restaurant section.

Poppy Red
The Arcadian Centre (0121) 687 1200
This construction site styled bar must have the most unusual dress code of any in town, with hard-hats and steel toe-caps compulsory for entry, and the music is an abstract industrialist noise. Oh I see. It's not actually open yet. By the time you're reading this though the workmen should be done and (hopefully) dusted and we'll have another stylish addition to Brum's bar and restaurant life. Hard to say too much at the moment but the owners are promising something special (as they would) so we'll keep our fingers crossed.

Sobar
The Arcadian Centre (0121) 693 5084
A more Manga-esque take on minimalism than a couple of the other Arcadian establishments, this cool and modern Japanese style noodle bar is an essential low light industrialist calling point if you're in the vicinity. There's a decent amount of outdoor seating for those summer months, when you can watch the buzzing activity of other bar hoppers in the area. The food is a bit pricey but highly praised, and besides – once you're feeling comfortable after a few bottles of Kirin you'll be reluctant to get up

Natasha, 22, Journalist

So where can I buy you a drink?
Bar Room Bar
You dancing?
Tiger Tiger usually
A romantic meal (with me)?
Le Petit Blanc or The Bank. I'm a classy lady
Favourite clothes shop?
Karen Millen (since closed down, though we expect it to re-emerge in the new BullRing in 2003)
What's great about Brum?
It's getting better all the time
You're telling me.

MORGAN'S SPICED
A MELLOW MIX OF SPIRIT AND SOUL
THAT FLAVOURS WHATEVER IT TOUCHES.

www.itchybirmingham.co.uk

and move on. The new Kaijo members bar upstairs is available for private hire.
Ho Fan beef and spinach £5.95
Happy hour 12-7pm 2 for 1 all draught, selected spirits, bottles and wines.
Open 'til 2am (may close early mid-week), 12.30 Sun

Broad Street Brindleyplace

All Bar One
The Waters Edge, Brindleyplace (0121) 644 5861
Shoehorning the word bar into a pun-tastic name isn't the cleverest of ideas, but ABO's real national success is based on a policy of inoffensiveness. Whilst they're almost always relatively pleasant places for a quiet(ish) drink, and the food is more than acceptable, you're hardly likely to rush here to celebrate your Ruby wedding anniversary or your recent lottery win.
Chargrilled ribeye steak with fries £9.95
House wine £10.80
Open late 'til 12 Fri-Sat.

top 5 for... Happy hours
1. B3
2. Indi
3. Casa
4. Key Largo
5. Sobar

Bar 2 Sixty
260 Broad Street (0121) 633 4260

Little attitude or atmosphere joined with utterly banal décor ideas and the genius policy of having the amps permanently cranked up to reduce your hearing to that of your aged relatives, all combine to make this a truly mediocre social venue. Is it the hideously garish dancefloor or the multitude of shots being downed which make the lads susceptible to a bit of passing-by groping? Whatever, excellent business idea boys.
Lamb shank £6.95
Selected drinks promotions at all times excluding after 8pm Fri-Sun
Open late 'til 2am Mon-Sat, Sun 12-12.30.

Brannigan's
196-209 Broad Street (0121) 616 1888
Mix up some desperate grannies, lecherous men and Kappa slappers, add a bit of Chesney Hawkes or Jason Donovan, shut everyone in tight with all the radiators on and, wallah! Brannigan's. With guest appearances by the aforementioned has-beens (or never really beens in Chesney's case), it remains very popular all week, especially

student night on Tuesdays. There are good drink offers sometimes, but you'll find that you'll be asking for water before anything else, as the need to pour a glass on your head far exceeds the need to pour a beer down your throat. All in all a cheeky, cheesy, cheerful place, but not worth getting all hot and bothered about.

Whole hog sizzler £7.25
H/hour: Selected drinks half price B4 9pm
Open late 'til 2am Mon-Sat,
12.30am Sun

Brooklyns Vodka Bar

Broad Street (0121) 643 2648

It's white, it's alright and it's good for a vodka night. Brand new to Brum is Brooklyn's – one of four new bars that's just opened up in this mini-stretch of Broad Street. We've yet to see what kind of crowd it'll attract, but we'd hazard a guess at pre-club party types, with a relatively laid-back vibe during the week, and a vodka-snorting mess of a crowd come Friday and Saturday nights. Bizarrely, Revolution vodka bar has just opened up as well, so B'ham's about to get a lot messier.

Happy hour: All day Sun-Wed, Thu-Sat 5-8, vodka shots £1
Open late 'til 2am Mon-Sat, 12.30 Sun

Casa

Brindleyplace (0121) 633 3049

This swanky bar is part of a chain that has taken cities across the country by storm, and it's the best place for a drink in Brindleyplace bar none. There's a lot of comfy seats (leather couches you'll never get up from), but it doesn't look cluttered. It's a smart bar, with attractive people, but it's not pretentious and there are no evil looking bouncers to scare you off. It makes a better alternative to

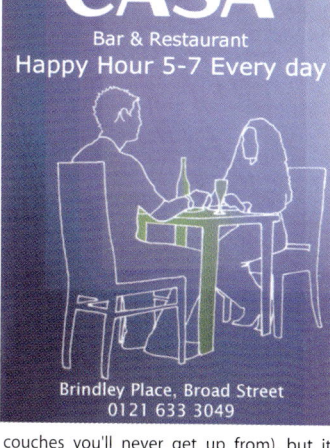

A MELLOW MIX OF SPIRIT AND SOUL.
THAT FLAVOURS WHATEVER IT TOUCHES.

www.itchybirmingham.co.uk

bars

the nearby options because of its chilled atmosphere. They serve good food too, mainly of the Italian variety and the dining area is separate too, so you don't feel hampered or rushed when eating. Unsurprisingly this has quickly become one of the most popular bars in town and it does get very lively especially at the weekends. Highly recommended.
Skewered ground lamb copidyka £5.95
Happy hour: 5-7 selected drinks offers.

Cube
Brindleyplace
What are you still doing here? What, I thought with your mass of drinks promotions, dubious decibel levels, and mish-mash of garish design you'd have cleared off by now? Well, if you're going to stay, you'll have to make up your mind – your pool table tells me you're a pub, your dance music makes you seem like a club, but I reckon you're neither. Now, either sort your act out or clear off, understood? Cheap beers makes it advisable to grab 'em, neck 'em and run.

Gio's
Paradise Circus (0121) 200 3801
People in glasshouses shouldn't throw stones, as the old saying goes, so I won't say too much in criticism of Gio's. At least not while I'm in it anyway. Kind of like a drinking greenhouse, they opted for the bar facelift to fit in with the rest of Broad Street. Not the kind of place you can imagine spending the whole night, but as a pit-stop for a night on the town, not half bad for a swift drink or a cheap bite to eat.
Steak and chips £3
Happy hour: selected drinks offers at all times.

Edwards
36 Broad Street (0121) 643 0444
The drinking equivalent of an Escher drawing, this maze-like bar will leave you dizzily confused after your sixth circuit, returning you back to the same spot you started in, and wondering how to get out. It's like a huge living room, but one that you'll have to share with the rest of Birmingham on a Saturday night. There's a small dancefloor and not a lot of seats, so it's usually standing

38 itchy**birmingham** 2002

room only – you can neck a few double house spirits and then traipse across the road to the Walkabout.
Bangers and mash £5.50
Happy hour 5-8 selected drinks offers.
Open late 'til 12.30 Fri-Sat

Grosvenor Casino Bar
Broad Street (0121) 631 2414
Vegas baby, Vegas. OK, put on the single-breasted pinstripe, break open the piggy bank, get out your membership card and hit the 'floor'. Actually, that's a 'dance' floor, the Casino is upstairs, but seeing as you're here you may as well take your chance to have a flutter at the bar and risk making a fool of yourself dancing to some 2-step. In a rather exclusive and classy place like this the prices are, as you'd expect, on the high side, but I suppose this just enhances the casino effect by leaving you completely empty pocketed by 2am.
Open late 'til 2am Mon-Sat

Hard Rock Café
263 Broad Street (0121) 665 6562
Well they picked the right place for it. In the heart of Broad Street with all the other brassy, in your face, theme-heavy chain bars. Rock and roll may be the motif, but swigging Jack Daniels from the bottle and snorting cocaine off the bar will be met with swift ejection (and possibly incarceration), and there isn't even a swimming pool around the back to park your 'Roller' in. At about £9 for a cheeseburger, Elvis impersonators are going to have to be prepared to stump-up around £180 for a meal fit for The King. Thankfully.

Henry J. Beans
Broad Street
Not open when we went to print, with construction work galore going on. But a brief peak inside revealed a great big map of America, in a glorified Yankfest. Whoo-hah!

Ipanema
60 Broad Street (0121) 643 5577

No need to 'pass by'. No need to 'go aah' longingly. Unlike the legendary girl from the similarly named Brazilian village, anyone adhering to the usual Broad Street dress stipulations can enter this place at will, and they probably should. A large and impressively modern styled bar, the South American theme here is mercifully restricted to the menus, and we're spared carnival dancers and tacky sombreros adorning the walls.
Torn rope (slow braised beef) £5.95
Open late 'til 2am Tue-Sat,
12.30 Sun, 12 Mon

A MELLOW MIX OF SPIRIT AND SOUL. THAT FLAVOURS WHATEVER IT TOUCHES.

www.itchybirmingham.co.uk

bars

■■ Key Largo
193-194 Broad Street (0121) 616 1300
'Aruba, Jamaica, ooh I wanna take ya to Bermuda, Bahama, come on pretty momma, Key Largo, Montego…' OK, so the Beach Boys probably weren't referring to this Broad Street bar in their underrated 80s comeback record, but with cheap booze and offers on cocktails, this is a decent stop-off point on any pub-crawl. However, if Brian Wilson were to pay a flying visit, his predilection for wearing a dressing gown and slippers in public wouldn't be met with the warmest of welcomes, as despite being one of the more casual bars along Broad Street, certain standards must be observed. Dance music, disco lights and dazzling bar – the only thing this place lacks on occasion, is people. With two floors and masses of room to hula, it has the unfortunate position of being next to Brannigan's and is often done out of a crowd. Come the weekend, as the students disappear, so do the drinks offers and it's frequented by the usual Broad Street posers, with eardrum blowing music.
Chicken balti £5
Open late 'til 2am Mon-Sat
Happy hour: selected offers before 6pm

■■ Mellow
192 Broad Street (0121) 643 5100
There's no chance of having this lot under the Trade Descriptions Act. 'A Ronseal' as we say at itchy: It does exactly what it says on the tin (sad isn't it). Infinitely more chilled than nearly any other bar along Broad Street, it's kind of like a prep school for Ronnie Scott's under-graduates. This might sound dull, and if you're a Merchant Stores regular you'll probably think it is, but in reality it goes to show that you don't need to bang out Euro-dance beats at ear bleed levels to attract a decent young crowd. Now surely that's a lesson that one or two bars round here would do well to learn.
3 course dinner £14.95 House wine £10.50
Open late 'til 1am Wed, 2am Thu-Sat

■■ Merchant Stores
Broad Street (0121) 633 4207

"Baby, we need to talk" she says, "It's about 'us'." "Of Course," he mutters, "Our relationship is important to me, let's discuss it over a drink." And so they simper off in uncomfortable silence, making small talk to pass the

itchy**birmingham** 2002

time 'til they reach Merchant Stores (his choice – him being the man and all). She sits down and lights a Marlboro Menthol while he goes to the bar and gets himself a pint and a spritzer for the little lady. She takes a deep breath as he returns to the table and pours out the last three years of disappointments and frustration. After twenty minutes of heartfelt emotion has flooded out, he looks at her and says "Sorry love, I can't hear a word you're saying with this bloody cranked up sound system."
2 meals for £6 (Scampi and chips)
Happy hour: selected offers Sun-Thu.

■■ MG's Pit Stop
Brindleyplace (0121) 644 5982
A question for Formula 1 buffs. What's the average time for a pitstop these days? Seven, eight seconds? Feels like an eternity to me. Fill pint, raise glass, open gullet, down beer. Clear. Right let's get out of this overrated bar and continue our circuit of Brindleyplace as soon as possible. It's a good location, overlooking the canal, but so are plenty of other bars these days, and it takes a bit more to stand out from the crowd.

■■ Old Orleans
80 Broad Street (0121) 633 9201
Have you ever been to New Orleans? No? Well that's probably what the proprietors are banking on if they're harbouring any pretensions of passing this off as authentic. Throw out the tacky memorabilia, knock out a few of the fluorescent lights, introduce a few murderers and drug dealers and then you'd be getting a bit closer to a true taste of the Deep South. That's the problem with modern life, there's just not enough risk is there? You could always introduce your own elements of danger though. Try chatting-up that drunken blonde's boyfriend. Start an impromptu game of cheeseburger frisbee. Go and drink that moustachioed man in the corners pint. In fact drop your pants and piss in it. Actually thinking about it, with this being Broad Street, that's all perfectly acceptable behaviour. How do you really offend people these days? Bring them here I suppose.
Steak sandwich £5
Happy hour: 3-7 selected drinks £1.50

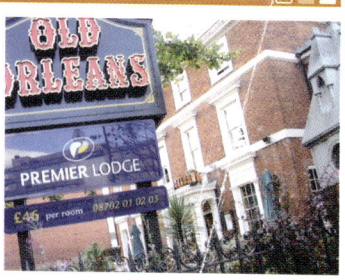

■■ Pitcher and Piano
Brindleyplace (0121) 643 0214
Posh pub or casual bar? Which ever, it could be a really nice place to go if it weren't full of posers. The tables and chairs are pushed to the side in the evening allowing them enough space to display their assets, but during the day, it serves sophisticated pub grub for reasonable prices and is situated

bars

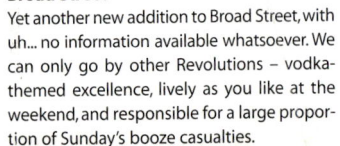

■■ Ronnie Scott's
Broad Street (0121) 643 4525
The fact that this is the accompanying bar/restaurant to what is one of the best-regarded jazz clubs in the country should give some indication as to the vibe of the place. Whilst it's not exactly full of chin-stroking cappuccino sippers, it certainly attracts a more mature and civilised crowd than many of the nearby alternatives.
2 course lunch £13.95 (Crab Louis)
Open late 'til 2am Mon-Sat 2am, 12am Sun

right by the canal, should you wish to throw yourself in there by the time the evening and the tossers arrive. Disregarding this unattractive crowd, the actual bar has a pleasant décor, with a roomy feel to it and toe-tapping music. A token piano in the corner serves to justify the name and add originality, though ultimately it fails, blending in with the rest of the show-off bars on Broad Street.
Pitcher & Piano burger £7.50

■■ Revolution
Broad Street
Yet another new addition to Broad Street, with uh... no information available whatsoever. We can only go by other Revolutions – vodka-themed excellence, lively as you like at the weekend, and responsible for a large proportion of Sunday's booze casualties.

■■ Sports Café
Broad Street (0121) 633 4000
The All England Lawn Tennis Club of sports bars, this place has a definite superiority complex and enforces a strict dress code that perversely outlaws all sporting apparel. Mystifyingly popular, this odd combination of sporting entertainment in what are otherwise fairly average bar surroundings is consistently packed with sharply dressed sports fans with varying standards of dancefloor athleticism.
Half chicken and rack of ribs £11.95
Happy hour: All day Sun. 5-2 Mon-Tues. All night Thu (student night). Selected drinks £1/1.50. Open late 'til 2am Mon-Sat

Tiger Tiger
Broad Street (0121) 643 9722

Places that try to be all things to all people are generally doomed to failure. As a combination venue of late bar, restaurant and nightclub, you'd expect Tiger Tiger to be a jack of all trades, master of none, but remarkably it just about pulls it off. The front bar area is impressive enough, but move through to the large lounge area or the club at the rear of the building and you begin to appreciate just how big this place is. A downside is that because it's a place for splashing your cash and acting flash it does get a few poncey fashionable types in there and it can be damaging to your overdraft if you make a night of it in here. See clubs
Honey Schzewuan duck breast £10.95
Happy hour: 5-7 different drinks promos each day. Open late 'til 2am Tue-Sat. Closed Sun-Mon.

Walkabout
240 Broad Street (0121) 632 5712

You'd think with all their sporting dominance the Aussie staff in here would have something to smile about, but alas no. I know the weather's crap, but cheer up a bit. Posing as an Australian surfers type bar, this places serves as a light relief for those fed up with the stuffiness of Broad Street. During the day, it resembles an Aussie hangout with a huge sports screen, good lager and healthy tucker. At night, it turns into a pumping bar full of hammered students and pervy old men taking over the newly extended dancefloor. The music is decent cheese and the décor is comfortable enough not to make you feel guilty about spilling drinks, unlike some of the other plusher venues nearby. For a hellish experience, dive downstairs to the downstair's dive, Surfer's Paradise.
Aussie burger £5.90
Happy hour: Sun-Thu all day and 5-8 Fri 2 for 1 most drinks.
Open late 'til 2am Mon-Sat, 12.30am Sun.

Wine REPublic
Centenary Square, Broad Street (0121) 644 6464

You are entering Centenary Square. You are beginning to feel tired. You want to sit down for a minute. This is the kind of hypnotic

A MELLOW MIX OF SPIRIT AND SOUL. THAT FLAVOURS WHATEVER IT TOUCHES.

www.itchy**birmingham**.co.uk

bars

effect that this part of town has on me. When the sun's shining, and people are all lounging around by the fountain it just doesn't seem right to go back to work, does it? Well not without nipping in to the Rep for at least a quick one overlooking the square. It may not be as cutting edge and ultra-cool as some recent Birmingham bars but it has got a soothing, relaxed vibe. The décor actually sits in a happy middle ground, without being either cold and minimal, or garishly over-the-top, and all in all it's a decent place for a quiet drink.

2 course meal £11.95 (Sirloin steak with mustard sauce)

Central

■■ B3
12-22 Newhall Street (0121) 236 7879
Like an all-encompassing stately pleasure dome for middle-aged business types and junior account managers. Fantastically average but the best thing about this place is that if you're trying to pull that fit new temp, it represents a three-strike opportunity:
1) Charm him/her over a spot of dinner.
2) No joy? Oh dear, OK, move on for drinks at the bar. C'mon you minx/stud, you can do it.
3) Loser! Still no joy? OK, now it's time to bust a move on the dancefloor in the club. By this stage they've got to be fairly hammered, so closing the deal should be a piece of piss.

Happy hour: 9.30-10.30 Fri. 8-10.30 Sat, all drinks £1.50 exc. main spirits
Open late 'til 2am Fri-Sat

■■ Bacchus
Burlington Arcade (0121) 616 7991
Situated underneath the Burlington Hotel, this medieval place caters for those who are looking for a little more sophistication than that offered in most Birmingham bars. How dimly lit, thrones for chairs and tapestry on the walls makes for a fantastic evening I'll never know – but it does. It probably wouldn't please the bank manager to stay here all night, but it's not the kind of place you'll be forced to rack 'em up and get 'em down. Not the place for raucous banquets or a night of debauchery, but you can get that anywhere along Broad Street.

Braised shank of lamb £10.95

■■ Bar Med
159 Corporation Street (0121) 200 1623

Has someone been messing around with the contrast? The only real similarity with this bar and the Mediterranean is the necessity for wearing shades, and that anyone without a deep rich tan is going to look positively ghoulish in comparison to their surround-

A MELLOW MIX OF SPIRIT AND SOUL. THAT FLAVOURS WHATEVER IT TOUCHES.

DRINK VODKA OR ELSE.

AND I WOULDN'T ARGUE IF I WERE YOU. 100 WAYS TO DRINK VODKA INCLUDING 30 UNIQUE FLAVOURS AND INFUSIONS. LATE NIGHT LOUNGIN' UNTIL 2AM ON THURSDAY, FRIDAY AND SATURDAY. FREE ADMISSION. HIP HOP/FUNKY BREAKS/R AND B/SOUL. VODKA HEAVEN IS REVOLUTION IS VODKA HEAVEN.

FIVEWAYS ○ BROAD STREET ○ BIRMINGHAM ○ ALL RIGHTS RESERVED

RƎVOLUTION®

ings. You can understand bar proprietors looking for an angle but we're not in Torremolinos and liberal splashings of 'sunflower yellow' and 'ocean blue' aren't going to change that fact. On the plus side, it's a good size and the food's pretty decent, and there are worse places to piss it up in when it's pissing it down outside.
Paella £7.95
Happy hour: 5-7 Mon-Fri all drinks £1.50.
5-1am Sat (student night) all drinks £1.50.
Open late 'til 1am Fri-Sat

Bennetts
Bennetts Hill (0121) 643 9293
Ah the classic Greco-Roman pseudo Victorian train station look, complete with pillars and checker-board flooring. Superb looking bar, which as we all know, was a former Natwest bank, so it's about time they stopped banging on about 'trendy wine bars' in their adverts – it's Natwest who converted all their bloody branches in the first place. Anyway, completely novel, with a slightly older, sophisticated feel, serving up reassuringly good food at decent prices.
Chicken tikka melt £4.20

Circo
6-8 Holloway Circus (0121) 643 1400
Roll up, roll up... see the monkey eat the badger and the lady covered in sequins jump onto the feet of the dwarf covered in custard powder. This bar may have been open since the mid nineties (oh, so long ago) but it's still really popular. Has the ringmaster been putting special medicine in the crowd's choc ices or has quality over quantity finally reigned supreme? Judging by the cool crowds, great music and top-tent nights, we think so.
Chicken stir fry £5.50
Happy hour: 5-8 Mon-Sat. All day Sun.
Selected drinks 2 for 1.
Open late 'til 2am Mon-Sat, 12.30am Sun.

IceObar
16-Hurst Street (0121) 622 6878
Just around the corner from the Arcadian Centre, this bar is eerily quiet during the week, only coming to life at the weekends. IceObar offers an impressive array of beers from around the world, but they are served, by unconcerned, lack-lustre bar staff, evidently bored by the infrequent desire for drinks from the few customers that haunt the vicinity. The handful of people that are seen to be drinking at the bar belittles the quality of this place. It's well lit, with comfortable seats and a decent amount of room to scour the area on the weekend. Well worth a look.

artificial intelligence

Available from Tesco, Waitrose and other leading wine and spirit retailers. Also available from Bar 38, Casa, Henry's, J D Wetherspoon, The Rat and Parrot, Via Fosse, RSVP and other independent bars and restaurants.

For more information call 020 8943 9526

www.seborabsinth.com

bars

■■ Medicine Bar
The Custard Factory, Gibb Street
(0121) 693 6333

It's official. Alcohol is good for you. And considering the amount I've consumed in the Medicine Bar in recent years then I must be just about ready to challenge Brian Jacks to a squat thrust contest. This is the antithesis of the sterile chain bar philosophy. It's cool, it's comfy, and it even looks a bit dirty. Wicked. Because this split-levelled venue is a bit rough around the edges the whole crowd seems laid back and at ease. There's a minimum of posing as people spill-out into the Custard Factory and lounge around on the floor drinking and talking the kind of nonsense that should be talked on Saturday night. The room next door also doubles as a club with some of the more eclectic nights in Brum – check itchybirmingham.co.uk for details.
Open late 'til 2 Mon-Sat

■■ Quo Vadis
190 Corporation Street (0121) 236 4009

Being in close vicinity to Birmingham's law courts, you regularly find legal types in here doing a 6 to 8 (pint) stretch after a days hard labour, although by the end of the evening most of them look completely incapable of finishing a sentence. The bar's a pretty standard mid-nineties design with the obligatory wooden tables and flooring. It doesn't really attract the fashion set, but it's a popular drinking destination for many. Whilst it does get busy, it never gets really boisterous, so save your drinking games and football songs for elsewhere if you don't want to upset the status quo.
Supreme chicken £6.50
Open late: 'til 12am Fri. 'til 1am Sat.

■■ RSVP
186 Corporation Street (0121) 236 1945

A refreshing bar, situated refreshingly outside Broad Street, RSVP occupies one of the

IT'S THE DREAM JOB.

48   itchy**birmingham** 2002

best spots in Brum. Resting on the edge of the town centre, this quiet little number serves a wide menu of Italian, Thai and English dishes up 'til about 8pm, when the lights are dimmed and the music gets louder. Attracting a mid-20s commuter crowd (presumably those who make a beeline from New Street Station), there's a feel good atmosphere here and what stands as a very decent restaurant (whose philosophy is; 'if there's something you don't like, we'll change it'), which turns into a bar with a dancefloor to keep you there 'til closing.
Thai grilled chicken £6.75
Happy hours: All day Tues, house wine £5. 5-7 Fri, House wine £5 and Pints of Heineken £1.50. Before 8pm Sat, vodka Red Bull £1.

Slug & Lettuce
17 Thorpe Street (0121) 622 5659
'I'd rather cut off my nipple and dance the Marshmallow than drink in here' Is what I'd like to say about all chains bars, but when, as in this case, they're quite good you can't really – which is a shame. If there is a hierarchy amongst chain bars, with Casa at the top and McClusky's at the bottom, then Slugs would generally be in the higher echelons. Nothing too remarkable, and you won't be surprised by the décor if you've been in any of their other bars, but it stays just this side of bland, which is a term that could never be applied to the food, which is a cut above most chain bar snacks.
Chicken fajita £4.50 House wine £10

Mailbox
The whole development around the Mailbox is still in an embryonic stage, but it is showing potential. Whether it'll ever be a socialising location in its own right remains to be seen, but it's a welcome oasis in the trail from the city centre to the Broad Street area even now. With the number of classy drinking and dining establishments growing and the potential custom of all those thirsty broadcasting types moving in, who knows what it could lead to.

Bar Room Bar
Wharfside Street, The Mailbox
(0121) 632 1199
Oh, ho ho ha ha , you witty little monkeys. It appears as though you were all at the same brewery board meeting when the big cheese suggested cramming a bar-based pun into the title of your establishment, for

BUT YOU DON'T WANT TO LOOK DESPERATE.

best spots in Brum. Resting on the edge of the town centre, this quiet little number serves a wide menu of Italian, Thai and English dishes up 'til about 8pm, when the lights are dimmed and the music gets louder. Attracting a mid-20s commuter crowd (presumably those who make a beeline from New Street Station), there's a feel good atmosphere here and what stands as a very decent restaurant (whose philosophy is; 'if there's something you don't like, we'll change it'), turns into a bar with a dancefloor to keep you there 'til closing.

Thai grilled chicken £6.75
Happy hours: All day Tues, house wine £5.
5-7 Fri, House wine £5 and Pints of
Heineken £1.50. Before 8pm Sat, vodka
Red Bull £1.

Slug & Lettuce
17 Thorpe Street (0121) 622 5659
'I'd rather cut off my nipple and dance the Marshmallow than drink in here' is what I'd like to say about all chains bars, but when, as in this case, they're quite good you can't really – which is a shame. If there is a hierarchy amongst chain bars, with Casa at the top and McClusky's at the bottom, then Slugs would generally be in the higher echelons. Nothing too remarkable, and you won't be surprised by the décor if you've been in any of their other bars, but it stays just this side of bland, which is a term that could never be applied to the food, which is a cut above most chain bar snacks.

Chicken fajita £4.50 House wine £10

Mailbox

The whole development around the Mailbox is still in an embryonic stage, but it is showing potential. Whether it'll ever be a socialising location in its own right remains to be seen, but it's a welcome oasis in the trail from the city centre to the Broad Street area even now. With the number of classy drinking and dining establishments growing and the potential custom of all those thirsty broadcasting types moving in, who knows what it could lead to.

Bar Room Bar
Wharfside Street, The Mailbox
(0121) 632 1199
Oh, ho ho ha ha , you witty little monkeys. It appears as though you were all at the same brewery board meeting when the big cheese suggested cramming a bar-based pun into the title of your establishment, for

BUT YOU DON'T WANT TO LOOK DESPERATE.

www.itchybirmingham.co.uk

bars

and laidback vibe. Despite its stylish appearance, it doesn't attract a really trendy crowd and subsequently is free of some of the pretension of other bars. It's not as lively or loud as your typical city centre drinking establishment but it's a good alternative because of it. Ideal for a coffee whilst doing a spot of afternoon shopping it does liven up in the evenings (and will do so even more once the BBC relocate to the Mailbox) but remains a pretty sophisticated experience.

QUINN'S
109 - 111 Wharfside Street
The Mailbox Birmingham B1 1RF
Tel: 0121 632 1474

It's a sign of how Birmingham's dragging itself into the 21st Century, that modern style bars like this can actually appear outside the city centre. Only a few years back this would have been thought of as revolutionary, even if it had been plonked in the middle of Broad Street, but in Moseley it would have been unthinkable, no... evil. In truth it's nothing remarkable, the decor's all been done before, but in relation to the competition around here it's as sophisticated as a smoked salmon and dill canapé on a silver platter, and makes a good old change to the chain boozers that surround it.

Chicken and bacon with pasta and white wine sauce £8.50

■■ Out Of Town

■■ The Cross Bar
Alcester Road, Moseley (0121) 449 4445
You could imagine ageing Moseley pub folk standing bewildered outside this bar like a scene from Close Encounters of the Third Kind. "Worrissit Stan, where'd it cum from?"

BEWARE OF THE VOICES. FOR CAREER ADVICE WORTH LISTENING TO, INCLUDING HELP WITH INTERVIEWS, VISIT monster.co.uk

www.itchybirmingham.co.uk

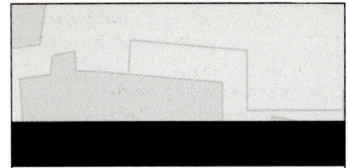

pubs

www.itchybirmingham.co.uk

We've carved up the city into handy pub-crawling areas. For more details about each section, see the introduction. Pubs open normal licensing hours unless otherwise stated, and if they serve food, we've put down the hours.

City Centre

City Centre: Aston Triangle

The Black Horse
Jennens Road, Aston Triangle
(0121) 359 7108
In its heyday, The Black Horse was full of punks and old chuffers with dogs on bits of string. Fights used to kick off on the hour, every hour, affectionately known as happy hour to the locals. How it's all changed. Nowadays, like dirty dishes and empty beer cans, wherever you find students, you're likely to find the ubiquitous 'It's a scream' chain. They've waded in and sanitised the pub with a liberal coating of lousy yellow paint, installed a few pool tables and lashings of drinks promotions. A brightly-coloured oasis in and amongst the bleak surroundings of Aston? Nah, roll on happy hour.
Food 12-7

■■ Gosta Green
Holt St, Aston Triangle (0121) 359 0044

Why stop at Edward Munch, why not do a chain of Francis Bacon inspired pubs with paintings of animal carcasses on the walls? Sod it, lets do a Damien Hirst and fill it with real animal carcasses. Anything but another 'It's a Scream' pub, please. OK, so it's not as bad as some, and it's a definite improvement on the Black Horse, but this is getting out of hand. Generations of university students are going to graduate with permanently scorched retinas due to the acid-inspired colour schemes in these places. There's a loosely termed beer garden too (concrete square), but once you've taken in the sights of sunny Aston you actually start to see the appeal of gaudily painted yellow tap rooms.
Food: 12-7

■■ Sack of Potatoes
**10 Gosta Green, Aston Triangle
(0121) 503 5811**

Not quite as student orientated as some of the other nearby pubs, so the pint-drinking locals don't get disturbed from their moaning about working life by half-drinking undergraduates moaning about student life. The pub itself is fairly small, with thankfully not a drop of yellow paint in sight, and there's a decent sized lawn area – alright, it's the Aston Triangle – but it handily doubles as a beer garden for chilling when the weather's fine. That other sack of potatoes, David Ginola, is not usually seen supping in here though.
Food Mon-Fri 12-7.30. Sat-Sun 12-3

■■ City Centre: Broad Street

■■ Brasshouse
Broad Street (0121) 633 3383

Are you (a) a borderline alcoholic, (b) a sex starved 40 year-old, (c) a walking jewellery shop, or (d) all of the above? If so, I'll save you some time right now. Don't bother reading on as you've found your nirvana right here. This is Broad Street at its tackiest and towniest best. Predatory middle-aged women who've had one/ten too many rum and cokes fight for bar space with equally inebriated would-be lotharios, whose fading charms are equalled only by their fading tans.
Food Sun-Thu 10-3, 5-8, Fri 10-10.30, Sat 10-12
Open Sat 'til 12

■■ Fiddle and Bone
1 Sheepcote Street (0121) 200 2223

Hold on a minute, this doesn't sound like Paul Van Dyke or Robbie Williams. The music policy may certainly be something of a departure from the overwhelming majority

A MELLOW MIX OF SPIRIT AND SOUL.
THAT FLAVOURS WHATEVER IT TOUCHES.

www.itchybirmingham.co.uk

pubs

Barrington, 38, Local govt. officer

When you're not busy refusing drinks licenses, what's your favourite bar? That's not my job, but Bar Room Bar or 52 Degrees rate highly
Whatever. And which club keeps government officials rocking? Fuel at Bonds
Not a club as such. But how about a restaurant? Denial
How about for a spot of shopping? Autograph, Love
What's great about Birmingham? The diversity
And what's not? The diversity. Think about it. **Deep, very deep.**

of nearby pubs and bars, but if you've had your fill of Ibiza trance or commercial chart music then the nightly live musical performances in the Fiddle and Bone may come as blessed relief. More than successful in providing a genuine alternative, this pub attracts an older crowd but that shouldn't necessarily be interpreted as dull or boring.
Food 12-10

▪▪▫ Figure of Eight
236-239 Broad Street (0121) 633 0917
Broad Street, fancy get-up and pricey drinks eh? Well, nearly everywhere bar the Figure of Eight. With double spirits for under £2 and large and tasty portions of food (most notably the Wetherburger), you're onto a winner – financially at least. OK, so the movers and shakers of Brum aren't going to be seen sipping on their bargain pints, but the place is still popular amongst an older clientele and students out on a mission to get hammered before stumbling onto Brannigan's or Walkabout. And sometimes, that's as cool as it ever needs to get. It has a long bar, but doesn't seem to get as busy as its New Street twin – 'The Square Peg'.
Breakfast 8am-10am, 9am-11 Sun. Lunch menus served all day.
Open 8am/9am for brekkie, but normal licensing hours for booze apply.

▪▪▫ The James Brindley
Bridge Street (0121) 644 5971
There was a quiet, mousy fella called James Brindley; millmaker by trade, but he turned his hand to canals and was pretty good at it. Apparently, so the history books tells us, he didn't say a great deal and loathed putting his plans or ideas on paper. So it seems nat-

54   itchy**birmingham** 2002

ural that in honour of our Jimmy that they didn't really have any plans when they built this pub. It's a bit... well, lacking in identity. But before you write it off, that's actually one of its plus points – sometimes the 'character-ful' pubs and bars of the surrounding Broad Street can be a bit full on. It's not heaving with pissed up yoofs or pounding with Euro trance beats, so it can't be too bad can it?
Food Mon-Fri 12-3, 5-7.30, Sat-Sun 12-4

The Malt House
Brindleyplace (0121) 633 4171
One of the better pubs around Brindleyplace and the canal area, it has a more traditional feel than most with your old rustic wooden beams and canal-side seating. It's usually quite relaxed and a comparatively peaceful place for an afternoon pint during the week, but that changes into an all-round disco-fest at the weekend when the tunes are cranked up, Bacardi Breezers are sold by the tart-load and Abba make yet another sodding revival.
Food 12-9. Open 'til 1am Fri-Sat

The Old Monk
230 Broad Street (0121) 633 3803
I'd be monked if I had to spend more than a pint in this undistinguished pub. Having no discernible identity it's little wonder this place hasn't got a prayer of attracting a loyal flock. Fairly muted during the week, when what little number of punters there are appear to have taken a vow of silence. Some life is injected at the weekend but there's still not really enough to recommend making a habit of it. In fairness the Old Monk was closing down for a refurb as we went to print, so we may have to re-assess.
Food 12-7
Planned late license after re-opening

O'Neill's
Broad Street (0121) 616 7821
These mock mick theme pubs have spread accross the country like a pack of marauding leprachauns, but begorah this is actually pretty good. Friendly bar staff (mostly Irish) serve you a jar of the black stuf and for once their shamrocks don't look like a pile up on Spaghetti Junction. There's a separate late-

A MELLOW MIX OF SPIRIT AND SOUL. THAT FLAVOURS WHATEVER IT TOUCHES.

www.itchybirmingham.co.uk

pubs

license music room attached, complete with wooden dancefloor, which the ever-persistent bar staff will encourage you to grace. Amidst the middle-aged crones all singing along to the old classics, there's a terrific atmosphere, where you can either sit back and laugh at the crowd (without getting your head punched in) or join in. The food is pretty good too, with authentic native dishes like soda bread, black pudding and Irish stew, satisfying the taste buds even though the majority of their punters are no more Irish than Jack Charlton.
Food 11-7 full menu
(restricted menu after 7)
Open Mon-Sat 'til 2am in the Music Room.

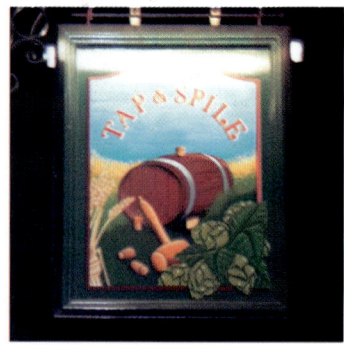

■■■ Tap and Spile
Gas Street (0121) 632 5602
It's not quite the traditional English country boozer (you are in the heart of the city you know), but it's pretty damn close. So, no old gents studiously involved in domino games with a whippet for company sipping pints of mild, but not too many Vodka Kick-swilling teeny boppers either. One of the few pubs in the area with some genuine character, making it ideal for kicking back and relaxing with a cold smooth pint.
Food Mon-Thu 12-3, 5-7.30, Sun 12-5.30.

■■■ City Centre: Central

■■■ Bier Keller
Royde House, Suffolk Place
(0121) 354 6652
Whether you're planning a putsch or a piss-up then Mr Bills is an essential calling point. Actually, you're better off just sticking to the piss-up, as, after a few steins of bier, you, like the rest of the mob in here will be about as capable of socio-political uprising as the present student population of the country.
Food served at all times.
Open Mon-Sat 'til 1.30am

■■■ Comfort Inn
Station Street (0121) 643 1134
Kind of depends on your definition of comfort really. If you still live with your mum and dad in a skeggy pit that hasn't been decorated in over a quarter of a century then you'll feel immediately at home in this bed and breakfast bar. Even if you've been stuck on the Midland Mainline for the last four hours with only a carriage full of Millwall fans for company and a £1.25 can of Coke for comfort, I'd still recommend the effort of straying a little further from the station for an essential nerve settling quencher.

The Crown
Hill Street (0121) 616 7801
An old mans pub in one of the ugliest parts of town, you're not going to find too many of Birmingham's trendsetters here. Brilliant. This unremarkable city centre pub potters along keeping its regular crowd happy by ignoring the gimmicks and gizmos so popular in other places. It's not a particularly friendly place for new faces, but as long as you keep yourself to yourself, you'll be fine.

Factotum and Firkin
23 Bennets Hill (0121) 631 3548
Located up a little side road from New Street, it's good for surrounding business people or tired shoppers to nip in for a swift half and a bite to eat – but not many make a special trip here in the evening. The pub has a lot to offer with its high ceiling (it used to be a church) and cosy upstairs seating, where you can look down and snigger about the bald heads below. That generally sums up the average age of the punters, and it's more the position of this pub that explains the absence of young people, rather than the actual place itself. There's a big screen for sports and tasty grub too. An undiscovered treat.
Food served 12-6.30

Hogshead
29 Newhall Street (0121) 200 2423
Hogsheads? Well they're better than Firkin pubs aren't they? No surprises here, in this clinically standard drinking venue with a good selection of drinks, reasonable food, and excellent levels of hygiene, which may not get you gibbering with excitement, but it's a perfectly decent place. The difference here is the clientele – largely suited and booted desk jockeys craving a couple of Belgian lagers after a hard day's duckin' and a divin', wheelin' and a dealin'.
Food served 12-9 Mon-Thur. 12-8 Fri-Sat.

Newt and Cucumber
58 Stephenson's Place (0121) 643 2969
American tourists may be fooled into thinking pub names like Newt and Cucumber have been all the rage since the days of

A MELLOW MIX OF SPIRIT AND SOUL. THAT FLAVOURS WHATEVER IT TOUCHES.

www.itchy**birmingham**.co.uk

pubs

Henry VIII but the rest of us know this utter nonsense is a recent thing. The complete absence of tradition isn't confined to the name above the door, as a plethora of fruit machines, video games and God knows what else, are in full attendance to violently remind you that this is indeed the modern world. Like the Rotunda, the Newt is a landmark (in terms of boozing) – steadfastly doing the job and revered by native Brummies for its simplicity and good honest pints.
Food served 11-7 Sun-Fri 11-11 Sat.
Saturday late license currently under review.

O'Neill's
The Arcadian Centre
(0121) 666 4951

The former Pat O'Connells maintains its Irish roots with this, a proper down-to-earth pub slap bang in the middle of the artsy, fashion-conscious and irritatingly expensive area of Hurst Street. For when a fancy bottled beer won't fill that pint-sized gap in your belly like a Guinness would, O'Neill's is a friendly, lively and top-notch pub in Brum. Deceptively large, and often host to live bands and a cracking atmosphere, we still fully recommend this pub as one of the best in Brum.
Food served 12-9 Sun-Thu, 12-12 Fri-Sat
Open 'til 12.30am Fri-Sat

Old Joint Stock
4 Temple Row West (0121) 200 1892

What came first, the chicken or the egg? Do suited business types really only want to drink in converted bank wine bars, or is it just because they're there? But it's not all hostile take-overs, and financial faux pas of Nick Leeson proportions... oh it is actually.
Food served 12-8.30

PJs Moon and Sixpence
Hurst Street (0121) 666 4941

I probably wouldn't call in here if I was cruising the Arcadian bars. I wouldn't come in if I was 'slumming' it round the corner in O'Neill's either. There's a pattern forming here isn't there? Utterly standard city centre pub-by-numbers, with suitably formulaic décor and an unselective crowd.
Food served 12-3

Sam Weller's
Hill Street (0121) 616 1731
Definitely the best pub in town, this is… Sorry about that. I've warned my dad before about using my typewriter.

The Shakespeare
Lower Temple Street (0121) 616 7841
'Is this a lager I see before me?' I can't understand a word of this Shakespeare lark. Or at least not the way the old schizoid sitting next to me at the bar was reciting it. To be fair, reciting sonnets and soliloquies wouldn't be too easy after twelve pints of Woodpecker even if you had your own teeth. Forget the Bard, the sign on the gents would be a challenging read to the average drinker in here.
Food served 12-7 Sun-Fr. 12-6 Sat.

Square Peg
115 Corporation Street (0121) 236 6530
This friendly pub is best for outrageously cheap drinks. Situated in the town centre, there aren't any clubs nearby to stumble to and the pubs and bars that surround it don't match these prices. As a Wetherspoon's pub, it boasts a no music and cheap booze policy and despite its recent refurbishment, the old men with their ale still come in their hordes, adding to the mixture of middle-agers 'out for a quiet one', and commuters 'out for a loud one.' Having the longest bar in Birmingham means you'll get to the front straight away, but be prepared for a long wait, as not surprisingly this gets very busy.
Food served 12-10 Sun-Thur.
12-9.30 Fri-Sat.

top 5 for... Watch the footy
1. Sports Cafe
2. Yard of Ale
3. The Toad
4. Walkabout
5. Gun Barrels

The Toad
16 Hurst Street (0121) 633 9584
The majority of the time this pub serves a purpose (and a damn important one at that). You want to watch the Blue's latest attempts to win the play-offs (they'll do it this year, I know it) or Villa striving for that coveted Intertoto spot, then this is the place. Big screens and tellies all over the shop, with an upstairs sofa spot that's nigh-on perfect for match days. Livens up in a pre-club way come the weekend, for a fairly townie but lively affair. Not half bad.
Food served 12-8 Mon-Sat 12-5 Sun
Currently applying for late license.

The Trocadero
Temple Street (0121) 616 2631
I preferred this place when it was a dump, but I'm clearly in a minority. The Trocadero has had just enough shine taken off it to make it feel a bit more genuine and relaxed than most non-traditional city centre pubs. It's a decent size and popular with a young but refreshingly unpretentious crowd.
Food served 12-8pm

MORGAN'S SPICED — A MELLOW MIX OF SPIRIT AND SOUL. THAT FLAVOURS WHATEVER IT TOUCHES.

www.itchybirmingham.co.uk

Yard of Ale
New Street (0121) 616 7901
Take a large dollop of character, add a colourful history, and place 20 feet underground below New Street. Leave it for a few decades, and you have the Yard of Ale; the perfect respite from the crowds outside. Often fairly busy, but it's all relative – at least there aren't any screaming kids and there's alcohol on tap.
Food served 11-6

City Centre: St Pauls

The Actress and Bishop
Ludgate Hill, St Paul's
(0121) 236 7426

Woah, check out the Jekyll and Hyde of Brummie pubs in. An after-work favourite with the smart suits most evenings during the week (though blissfully free of wheeler-dealing banter) and come the weekends – well, hello, what's happened? A mature crowd come bouncing in and throw disco shapes like they were about to be denied the right to boogie. Good on 'em I say. The bizarre mix of folk suggest that there's definitely truth in the rumours about the actress getting jiggy with the bishop.
Open late 'til 1am Thu-Sat. Closed Sunday.
Food served 12-9

The Ropewalk
St Paul's Square (0121) 233 2129
This pub is murder during lunch hours from Monday to Friday. Not that it's anything special; all the nearby places are similarly packed out with city workers on a liquid lunch. The hardcore office party animals make it back for another pint after about five thirty, but the rest of the time it's pretty quiet (and far more bearable for it).
Food served 12-9 Mon-Sat. 12-3 Sun

The Jam House
3 St Paul's Square (0121) 200 3030
Bar, or pub or restaurant or club. Who knows what to call it, but Jools Holland has definitely done something right. (See clubbing review). As a pub/bar, it's a fine place for an afternoon pint or a bite to eat. Like many of the places around St Paul's it's fairly quiet during the day, when you can pretty much have the place to yourself, although I would

BIRMINGHAM'S BEST DANCE AND R&B

Galaxy 1022
www.galaxy1022.co.uk

resist the temptation to get on stage and lay down a few air guitar riffs. Fills up in the evenings with a mix of music fans of varying ages.
Open late 'til 1am Mon-Fri, 2am Sat.
Food served at all times.

■■ Selly Oak

■■ Bristol Pear
676 Bristol Road (0121) 414 9981

op tip: Students! When brandishing your 's a Scream' discount card, be sure to flamboyantly exclaim your delight at receiving ne same drink as your neighbouring skinhead punter for 20% less, as the locals find nothing funnier than the disparity between their well-earned wages and your seemingly endless supply of Home Counties cash. Housing a cramped mixture of pool tables, fruit machines, locals and students, the place heaves like a beached whale during term time, and like a washed-up squid during the holidays. Much like its sister The Gun Barrels, but with a less exclusively student crowd.
Food 12-7 Mon-Sat 12-6 Sun
Currently applying for late license.

■■ The Brook
Bristol Road (0121) 414 9911

"Ahh, bloody students. Yeah, go on, piss off with your fancy degrees and posh parents. You what? You want to use the pool table? No you frigging can't, haven't you got lectures to go to? Oh, I get it, you want to lounge around in the beer garden, chatting with your poncey mates telling everyone about your 'hilarious' tales with traffic cones. Well, you're not welcome. Yeah, that's right, and the back room's out of bounds too. But hold on. Don't all go. No, Christ, some of you can stay. Stop! Who's going to pay the bills? WAIT! Ahh shit, looks like they've gone for good."
Food 12-2.30 and 6-7.50
Sun-Thur 12-8 Mon.

■■ The Goose at the O.V.T.
561 Bristol Road (0121) 472 3186

From the Varsity Tavern, to the Firkin to the current Goose, this place has had many an unnecessary facelift. Especially this one – vomit inducing old people's home carpet replete with bookshelves to give that authentic library feel, helped by a strictly no-

A MELLOW MIX OF SPIRIT AND SOUL THAT FLAVOURS WHATEVER IT TOUCHES.

www.itchybirmingham.co.uk

music policy. And just for added authenticity, the hoary old scroats from the Brook have settled in and show no signs of moving, though unlike a library, they're nursing pints of mild and chuffing on pipes. But no matter – because it's next to the uni, this place is always busy with a lively student crowd. And because of the obscenely cheap prices – think of something cheap and then imagine a short stint in Bryan's 99p shop – you can't move for penny pinchers. Cheap then.

The Gun Barrels
Bristol Rd (0121) 471 2672
Gun Barrels equals Birmingham University. The Goose gets its fair share of students, but here, there's practically nothing but. 'It's a scream', naturally, but don't fear. It's really quite good. Filled with nothing but up-for it revellers, it's loud, brash and lively. You'll probably save a few quid at the weekend too, thanks to cheap drinks and the 25-minute wait at the bar. Supposedly the highest grossing pub in the country, you've got your pool tables, decent-sized beer garden and blindingly bright décor. I often wondered what Bananaman was doing since his days on Acacia Street and now I know… Interior designer for the almost exclusively student 'It's a scream' chain.
Food 12-7pm Sun-Sat.

TC's
Coronation Road (0121) 472 0939
More like a social club than a conventional pub, this is possibly the best drinking venue in Selly Oak. With pool tables and a function room it's got a relaxed friendly atmosphere, and is probably the best place in the area for a quiet pint. You do get a fair few students in, but they tend not be the annoying attention seeking type, so they mix with locals without incident. Hosts the odd disco, plenty of private parties and occasional football/rugby matches.
Members only, though membership is free
Food served 'til 9.30

Harborne

Yes, yes, yes, the Harborne run is still illegal. You're still not supposed to drink from the far end of Harborne working your way to Selly Oak towards the White Swan/Dirty Duck, so just knock it off will you? And if you were to be so rebellious as to give it a go, just remember it's a pint or a double spirit in each. Bonus points for premium lager, minus points for any vomiting, and police points for fighting. This is just a selection of the pubs round here – there are much, much more than this.

■■ The Bell
11 Old Church Road (0121) 427 0934
If you're into bowls, this is the place to visit. You'll be regally entertained by the thrilling live action that takes place on the arena next to the beer garden. In fact this place is a veritable feast of sporting opportunity, with the outdoor toilets doubling up as a swimming pool and the ridiculous time it takes to get served at the two foot wide bar offering the perfect atmosphere for fighting to start. Except this is bowls, so steady on old boy, and a little less aggro if you don't mind.
Food 12-2.30 and 5.30-8 Mon-Fri.
12-3 Sat-Sun

■■ Fallow and Firkin
359 High Street (0121) 426 1048
'Pull cord and retreat to safe distance' – so read your instructions on your inflatable Firkin pub-in-a-box kit. Boring, boring, boring. It makes you wonder why they bother with these anodyne sanitised refurbs. If you've ever been sceptical as to the point of these places, then this example of the Firkin chain should compound your fears. Why here? Why anywhere for a place like this? I can't even be arsed to describe it to you; it's just like all the others.
Food served 12-2 and 5.30-8

■■ The Green Man
2 High Street (0121) 427 0961
The most common starting point for the Harborne run, it's a greatly improved pub since its renovation. Although it still lacks a pool table, there is more music and laughter than most of the pubs in the area. It's well decked out, boasts consistently good food and plenty of sofas to relax on. The contrast between this and the Sportsman is obvious, without a sad man to be seen, let alone a corner of them.
Food 12-8

■■ Harborne Stores
109 High Street (0121) 427 0971
The decision to 'splash out' on a pool table and jukebox was obviously at the expense of every other facet of the pub. Most notably the wallpaper (a tasteful, coffee stained paisley colour with more than a sprinkling of mould). The jukebox pumps out decidedly 80's tunes and after a couple of drinks, the mould does become a beautiful Aquamarine. Basically, if you're a squatter who loves playing pool whilst listening to Wham, Bon Jovi and Bananarama you're onto a winner.

MORGAN'S SPICED
A MELLOW MIX OF SPIRIT AND SOUL.
THAT FLAVOURS WHATEVER IT TOUCHES.

www.itchy**birmingham**.co.uk

pubs

■ ■ ■ The Sportsman
Metchley Lane (0121) 426 0941
Answers on a postcard as to why this place is called 'The Sportsman'. Does a solitary hunting picture really warrant such a title? It can't be the place the local sports teams go for post match chat as you couldn't even fit a five-a-side team of dwarves in here. Maybe the extremely attractive barmaid was the 1973 Hungarian Shot Putt Champion? With a general smuggler's tavern type feel, other features include lanterns, lots of wood and even a sign for 'sad mans corner'. You will probably get a strong urge to sit by it if you come here for a drink. Still, if you are doing the Harborne run, this place will get you off to a good start as you'll want to get the alcohol down your gullet quick smart so you can get on to one of the much better pubs in the area.
Food 6-8.30

■ ■ ■ The Plough
21 High Street (0121) 426 0924
With the finest slide in Harborne, and a unique whale seesaw, the beer garden is clearly the highlight of the Plough, being as it's twice the size of the interior, which resembles an old style bookies or possibly Sweeney Todd's barber shop. Beware of the agro crowd. Average age 75. But still 'ard.

■ ■ ■ The Varsity
186-192 High Street (0121) 426 4256
The inspiration for this place was surely the Crystal Maze, with large pipes adorning the ceiling purchased from the industrial zone. Apart from these evil lizard like forms that sit eerily above you the place is pretty smartly decked out with a big, square, central bar not dissimilar to the one used in Cheers. It attracts a young trendy crowd and makes a decent enough stopping point on the Harborne run.
Food served: 12-10 Sun-Thu. 12-7 Fri-Sat.

■ ■ ■ The White Horse
2 York Street (0121) 427 6023
Whichever way you look at it, £2.20 a pint is decidedly city centre prices, especially for a small place tucked off the main road, where you would expect to see the occasional guest beer at 90 pence a pint. Just about the darkest lung of a pub in Harborne the chairs and gym style wooden floor give it a sense of backwardness that couldn't be achieved anywhere apart from here. The image of Harborne pubs as a group of Sherwood Forest Taverns unfortunately continues.

IT'S THE MD

top 5 for...
Outdoor drinking
1. The Malt House
2. Bar Room Bar
3. Sobar
4. Denial
5. The Bell

Moseley

The Bull's Head
St Mary's Row (0121) 449 0586
The Bull's Head? The Bull's arse more like. Funny barmaids in an inbred kind of way. The bar itself is nasty, the beer is expensive and I'd rather eat by testicles than call this my local. There's an eclectic mix of weirdoes and locals (usually one and the same). No food, obviously, if there was I wouldn't bother. Don't even risk the crisps. In fact don't risk the pub.

The Goose @ The Fighting Cocks
St Mary's Row (0121) 449 0811
The Goose could be presented as evidence in the case of the chain pub vs culture. Who thought that the decor of bookshelves and photos of 100-year old streets would get everyone gibbering with excitement? Hey? And yes, we were all sick of all-wooden pubs, but I didn't hear a petition go round for a minging carpet, did you? The pub serves up cheap pints and food to a local older crowd, and despite the chain's attempt at squeezing every last drop of character from the venue, the clientele bring it up just a couple of notches. Only a couple mind.
Food 12-9

The Hogshead
Salisbury Buildings, Alcester Road (0121) 449 3340
A bit wooden in both décor and personality, this is a fairly typical, if uninspiring Hogshead pub. They're never too bad though, and this one is fine for a pint or two, but I never feel comfortable enough to make a night of it here. Not as smart as the majority of HH pubs, it's still smarter than most of Moseley, although that's lost on the older members of the crowd, who'd be happy enough drinking in an out-house as long as it got them away from the missus for the evening.
Food 12-9 Mon-Sat. 12-8 Sun

SHOW HIM YOU'RE NOT INTIMIDATED

www.itchybirmingham.co.uk

pubs

Jug of Ale
43 Alcester Road (0121) 449 1082
Hallelujah. A pool table in Moseley. Pumping tunes and swivel chairs give this place a real party atmosphere. Guaranteed to make the most conservative bounce along. Attracting a young, kinda-like-to-be-a-Goth, but not quite got the balls type crowd. The pub also doubles up as a washing line, so look out for the sheet that's been put up to dry. No review would be complete without mentioning the live music, Wednesdays, Fridays and Saturdays, where local bands get to grips with an up-for-it crowd, trailing in the glory of the once legendary Clemency who graced these amps many moons ago.

O'Neill's
93 Alcester Road (0121) 442 3901
No, you won't find a real flavour of Ireland. They'll be no shamrocks, riverdance, blarney stones or even leprechauns in this place. And they'll try and trick you with the Irish sounding names on the menu, such as the 'traditional Irish dish' Colcannon, which is uncannily like Bangers and Mash. But frankly, who gives a toss when the atmosphere is lively, good-natured, and there's bar staff doing table service. Moseley crowds are in their element here, and it's all the better for it.
Food 12-10 Sun-Fri. 12-8 Fri-Sat

Patrick Kavanagher
Woodbridge Road (0121) 449 2598
Character, crowd, atmosphere, beers and events. You couldn't ask for much more from a pub. If it was a dog, it'd win Crufts. If it was a singer, it'd win the Mercury Music Prize and if it was a drug den (as it was), it'd sell the purest crack in town (it doesn't and it's not, before skag-heads go running through the doors). The tiny upstairs room, S2, previously host to some drum'n'bass nights is dabbling with some comedy, and the main room is

JUST KEEP SMILING AT HIM

talking about serving food any minute now, reputed to be straight from the nearby Lime & Chilli house. Good work all round.
Food served 12-7 (Lime & Chilli House)

■■ Prince of Wales
118 Alcester Road (0121) 449 4198

It feels a bit tight to say it's tatty from the outside, and tattier still on the in (it is). Why? Because it's full of some of the most genuine people in town, serves cracking beer and has top quality bar staff. There's a decent beer garden round the back, living room type affairs behind the bar, and a genuinely relaxed and open atmosphere without a sniff of pretension.

■■ The Village
Alcester Road (0121) 442 4002
A pub of two halves. Seemingly seedy in the dirty front room, it expands in a tardis-like fashion into an admittedly old-school, but classy room at the back. With a cosmopolitan multicultural feel about the front bar and a decidedly local atmosphere in the lounge, this renovated nursing home is now nursing a wide mix of Brummie drinkers. Spacious, yet understated, with the smallest 'big' screen you will ever witness situated so high in the rafters you will leave with a seriously sore neck. The white kid bitching Slim Shady last year has now progressed to soft rock on karaoke nights too, so be warned. Look out for the leather padded thronal chair custom made for 80 year old, grey bearded pipe smokers.
Food 12-8.30

itchy sms @
www.itchybirmingham.co.uk

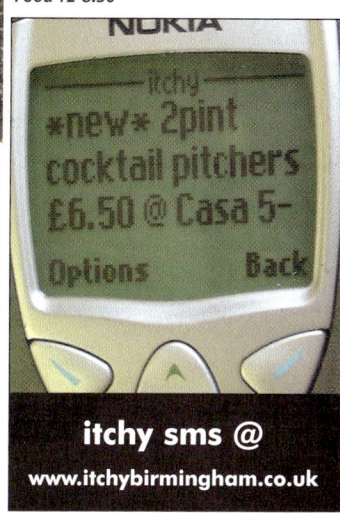

BEWARE OF THE VOICES. FOR CAREER ADVICE WORTH LISTENING TO, INCLUDING **HELP** WITH **INTERVIEWS**, VISIT monster.co.uk

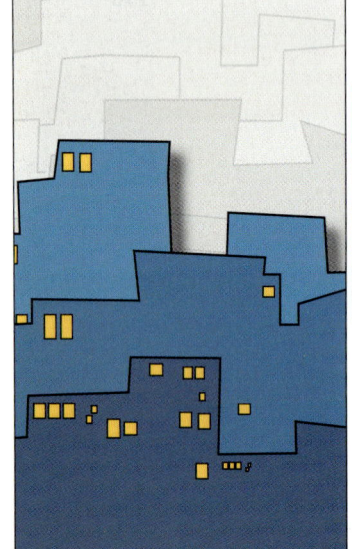

■■ The Academy
Dale End (0121) 262 3000

With the days of the Hummingbird nothing but a hazy, drug-fuelled, debauched memory, The Academy has moved on, taking its rightful stage as the place for decent bands to pay homage to this great city (I presume that's why they come, right?). Proving that you don't need glow-sticks, dancers and Class A's to have a thumping good night, the Academy is still resisting selling its soul to the dance devil. Live music revolves around some of the biggest and best bands touring round the UK, whilst club nights are strictly indie and the student tack-fest of Pump on Monday nights. Nothing fancy here, just 2000 people having a good time.

■■ Bakers
163 Broad Street (0121) 633 3839

In the Birmingham clubbing scene, names and nights change often but a common factor is that if you like your house hard and your dancefloor heaving you're generally well-served in the second city, and Bakers is usually to the fore of the scene. Still, considering how ridiculous anyone looks drenched in sweat reaching for the skies with that gurning look of ecstasy/constipa-

Finger tips

RIZLA+ It's what you make of it.
www.rizla.com

tion on their faces, it's ironic that you've got to look the part before you're allowed into many glam house clubs, and nothing changes here. Not a massive venue by any means, but style, atmosphere and beats are all served up regularly in king-sized portions.

■■ Bobby Brown's
48 Gas Street (0121) 643 2573
Having been open for over a decade this sizeable two-roomed venue hardly qualifies as a new edition to the Birmingham scene, but its enduring popularity ensures its inclusion here. Bobby Brown's hasn't seen any major changes in the ten years it's been open, choosing rather to work to the old adage of 'if it ain't broke don't fix it'. In fact they've even expanded on this ethic to encompass the advice 'don't decorate it, or even clean it too often either.' Aiming squarely at the middle-ground, this club has no pretensions of being something it's not; it just serves up the old staples of commercial dance music and plenty of booze to cross-generational shag-happy piss-heads. No doubt it will continue to do so long after the latest generation of suburban double garage or inflatable speed house nights have all been and gone.

■■ Bonds
Hampton Street (0121) 236 5503
Given the reputation for a strict dress code I looked at the name of this club and misguidedly thought that full tuxedo would be de rigeur. Imagine my embarrassment as I was unceremoniously excluded in full view of all Birmingham's beautiful people. This is a house club and as such the essential look is pure glam, baby. The insistence on the crowd looking outrageous and glamorous is probably a sly way of masking the fact that the venue itself is pretty ordinary. But that's not really important as long as the crowd and the music is bang on the money.

■■ Code
**Heath Mill Lane, Digbeth
(0121) 693 2633**
This ambitious development was clearly intended as a shrine to dance culture. The seating area and balcony are very much on the periphery of the really important stuff; the dancefloor. In refreshing contrast to many of Brum's leading venues, there's less emphasis placed on the way people look than the way they enjoy themselves. The sound system absolutely bangs and the

Hot tip

lighting rig is impressive enough to nearly induce epilepsy in all but the most hardened clubbers. Relaxing it's not, and there's more 'love' in the room than romance, but if you're just looking to lose yourself in the hardest of house beats, then God's Kitchen on Fridays is the night for you.

■■ DNA
John Bright Street (0121) 633 7456
DNA is certainly more music-led than your average corporate clubbing affair, but it's also less exclusive than most dedicated dance clubs, and therefore less attitude. Probably something to do with the size – there aren't enough pretentious tossers in Birmingham to fill it. Well, whatever the reasons for the atmosphere in the place, it can be a real good night, especially when it's busy. The place has got a bit of a science fiction vibe to it, complete with the UFO bar area floating above the main dance arena.

■■ Hidden
Wrottesley Street (0121) 455 9487
Any house-heads out there looking for a more grown up clubbing experience than that on offer at most of Brum's rather full-on hard house clubs should be sure to seek out this stylish new venue. In truth, Hidden won't be particularly difficult to find, as the masses of queuing clubbers around Wrottesley Street should probably give the game away. Those familiar with the Steering Wheel will be surprised, and almost certainly impressed, by the extensive renovation of this three-floored club. The new look is more plush and luxurious; with deep moody colour schemes and plenty of lounging/ligging space in the bar area. The intention is to unify a clubbing experience with more of a bar culture vibe but you can still expect some hardcore dancefloor action in the main room which is set to host some of the biggest names from the international DJ circuit. Still early days for this venue but it looks primed for success.

■■ The Hush
55 Station Street (0121) 242 6607
07939 954 592 membership details
Under stress? Too much caffeine in your diet? Worried about work? Maybe there's a

RIZLA+ It's what you make of it.

www.itchybirmingham.co.uk

completely different reason altogether why you'd still be wide awake at 4am on a Sunday morning, I obviously couldn't comment, but if you haven't had enough come closing time then The Hush is just about your only option. Most places that open at 2am are generally on the seedier side of the tracks, but this is no back-street drinking den (it doesn't even sell booze). The Hush is here to keep the night alive, whether you've still got your dancing shoes on or you just can't take the risk of going home and waking your mum up until you've chilled out a bit.

■■■ Flares
55 Broad Street (0121) 632 5501
The name's undoubtedly a reference to the style of trousers but I'm actually getting the word 'emergency' in big letters. Proudly positioning itself as a 70s club, this is an appropriately gaudy shrine to the decade that taste forgot, although at the old John Bright location, you'd have been forgiven for thinking it was an over 70s night looking at some of the crowd. Still, they've moved, and not all of the punters have followed suit, so its sassy new Broad Street address may well attract the Ipanema punters. I said may.

■■ The Jam House
3 St Paul's Square (0121) 200 3030
In a city that is surprisingly lacking in the way of live music, Jools Holland's Jam House goes a long way to redressing the balance.

Whilst there is a dress code, the bouncers are much less sub-human than the Nazi-like monkeys who prowl about outside the venues on Broad Street. The Jam House also boasts an extremely rare species – a female bouncer baring no resemblance whatsoever to Fatima Whitbread. Although it's a fiver to get in before 11 and seven quid thereafter (with drinks priced at the higher end of the scale) you definitely get your money's worth. Jazz pianists don't just tinkle but bash out lively, boogie woogie tunes until their fingers fall off. Then on come the band who pump out everything from Pink Floyd to Van Morrison. Although by night it's one big, fat energy ball, by day it's a relaxed bar come restaurant. Attracting a slightly older crowd, the weekend atmosphere is second to none.

Flick through the papers

itchy**birmingham** 2002

■■ Liberty's
184 Hagley Road, Edgbaston
(0121) 454 4444

If the majority of clubs seem permanently stuck in youthful delinquency then Liberty's feels like a nightclub that has passed through its cider swilling puberty and come out the other side pretty much unscathed. Safer and more civilised than the city centre alternatives, the place manages to stay looking fairly plush thanks to the fact that the more mature crowd it attracts doesn't seem overly prone to vomiting on the carpets or spilling alco-pops on the dancefloor.

■■ McClusky's
53 Smallbrook, Queensway
(0121) 616 3939

'This is a drug free venue' says the sign outside. Drug free? Personally I'd need to be off my mash on ecstasy pipes to even contemplate looking through the window of this dump. Once inside, it is indeed like a bad trip. Grotesque faces come out of the shadows. Hideous colours and shapes clash nauseatingly. Don't worry it's not you. It's a tragic reflection on the state of the nation that this chain of tacky American themed bar/club/restaurant venues is growing. Couldn't we at least have abysmal English themed clubs instead? Awful.

■■ Moseley Dance Centre
572-574 Moseley Dance Centre
(0121) 449 0779

"This club, it's not ready yet. What do you think you're doing? The floor, it hasn't been sanded, it's a school hall floor. You must coat it to make it a dancefloor. And wait, these chairs, these are not clubbing chairs. These are school chairs, for school children. The DJ booth my friends, that is not a booth, that's a school stage with a disco box and flashing lights suitable for only the crummiest of weddings. This music – oh stop stop stop, it's a mish-mash of 80s and 90s classics, not real clubbing music. And hold up, these punters – these are not clubbers, these are post-pub piss-heads. You must allow the elements to mature before you can call this a club". We'll let you know when it's ready.

Laura, 18, Student

And your favourite bar is...
Hard to say really. Bar 2 Sixty?
I don't know, is it? How about a club?
Stoodi's I think.
Are you sure about your favourite restaurant?
Caspian. At the moment anyway.
OK, something easier. Favourite shop?
Easy – Jane Norman.
Best thing about this second city?
The nightlife, definitely.
And the worst?
The weather.

RIZLA+ www.rizla.com

■■ Mustard
100 Watson Road, Star City
(0121) 327 2625
The Star City entertainment complex still hasn't really set the world alight with its attempt to create a little Vegas-styled leisure oasis on the M6. Unsurprisingly, Mustard is a fairly corporate clubbing affair that's got its work cut out in keeping people keen enough to continue coming out from the centre of the city. As you'd expect in this kind of development, the club is slick and smartly done out, but it's not really extreme enough in any direction to really command a loyal customer base.

■■ The Que Club
Central Hall, 212 Corporation Street
(0121) 212 0550
When naming this venue all those years back the proprietors where obviously anticipating it to be popular. They were of course right. The Que club has hosted some of Birmingham's most famous and infamous nights in recent times and it's probably the best-known venue in the city for all things house, techno and dance. Presently the big Saturday night event here is Atomic Jam, which continues the tradition of full-on dancefloor carnage throughout the three rooms of the club, throwing drum and bass and hip hop breaks in with the essential 4/4 beats.

■■ Ronnie Scott's
258 Broad Street (0121) 643 4525
There was a time when going to a nightclub didn't necessarily mean doing permanent damage to your eardrums and didn't require a visit to a council estate chemist beforehand. Ronnie Scott's harks back to a gentler more civilised time. A time before hard house, before glow-sticks. The patrons of this club are every bit as passionate about their music as any Broad Street raver, it's just that the music of choice in here is jazz, and all of a sudden, I find myself blowing smoke rings. You can drink and dine whilst soaking up the laid-back ambience and listen to live music from some pretty big names from the world of jazz and blues.

■■ The Sanctuary
Digbeth Street (0121) 246 1010
This massive cathedral-esque venue is another club that's been involved in the shake-up of Brum's club scene in recent years with some of its high profile nights moving on to other locations. The layout of

Hand book

74   itchy**birmingham** 2002

clubs

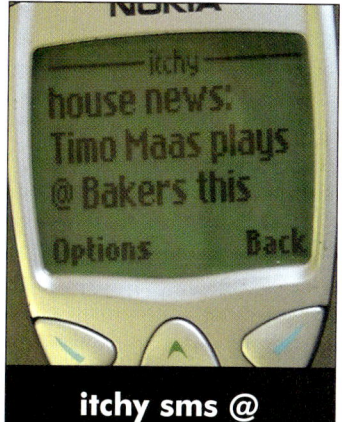

the club lends itself perfectly to the big hardcore dance events. It's set over three floors with a main dance arena, a mezzanine balcony and a chill-out and bar area. Nothing particularly drastic has been done to disguise its theatrical past, other than to paint the whole place red which helps make it feel less cold and cavernous.

■■ Snobs
**30 Paradise Circle, Queensway
(0121) 643 5551**
Snobs, which is full of anything but, attracts a fiercely loyal following of inebriated indie kids. Which must come as something of a blessing to the owners, who know that expensive renovations, or sod it, even a lick of paint would only serve to distress the crowd determined that the place stick to its roots and original decor. No dress code as such, though shiny-shoes, bright shirts and white stilettoes may raise a few eyebrows, especially if worn together. Two rooms serving up 70s, 80s, pop and indie keep the young crowd bouncing year after year.

■■ Stoodi Bakers
Broad Street (0121) 643 5100
An intoxicating cocktail of all that Broad Street embodies. Take a handful of cool cats and posers, add a couple of drunken douche bags and a few scrubbed-up students. Mix in a healthy spoon of commercial dance and finish with a liberal splash of pure alcohol and you have yourself a 'Stoodi Baker'.

■■ Surfers Paradise
**Underneath Walkabout, Broad Street
(0121) 632 5712**
Those Walkabout people can't be praised highly enough for once actually injecting some authenticity into one of their Aussie-themed venues. Forget the fact that it's raining outside and you really could be in some filthy drinking pit in the arsehole of the Australian outback. As an outsider, you'll marvel at the way they've captured the feeling of intimidation and alienation. Of course the crowd play along like some bizarre form of participation theatre with all the women looking like complete dingos and the guys all acting like flamin' gallahs. The only slight failing is the absence of any boomerang effect that might encourage you to return.

RIZLA+ It's what you make of it.

www.itchybirmingham.co.uk

clubs

top 5 for...
Places to pull

1. Zanzibar
2. Snobs
3. Stoodi Bakers
4. Bobby Brown's
5. Jam House

■■ Tiger Tiger
Broad Street (0121) 643 9722

Is it a bar? Is it a club? No, it's a sort of bar-club-restaurant combination type thing. The over 25s venue has now taken solid roots in Brum, but don't be fooled by the age policy. Unlike the majority of scuzzy places that use over 25s as a euphemism for haggard old crones, this is a smart and sleek venue with a late twenties crowd, drinking bottled beer on the top floor, bottled beer on the ground floor, bottled beer in the club, bottled beer in the tiger-striped sofa bar... you get the idea. Huge, multi-themed (ie, it's like several bars, club, restaurants that all happen to attach together) and style-conscious, the impressive scale of the club justifies an expectation for the punters to make a comparable effort.

■■ The Tower
**Reservoir Road, Edgbaston
(0121) 454 0107**

This is a proper throwback to old-skool nightclubbing. The 'Shower' is a strictly over 25s nightclub (as in age, rather than average consumption of Bacardi Breezers) and has a 'very strict' dresscode. This term basically translates as no trainers or jeans regardless of the value or style, whilst patent leather slip-ons and vinyl mini skirts will be more than welcome. The place claims, rather ambiguously, to be suitable for singles and couples, but take our word for it, the only swinging that'll be going on is when you start chatting up the wrong person, and their socially challenged other half starts swinging for your head.

■■ XLs
**Auchinleck Square, Five Ways
(0121) 643 9433**

The Friday night queues for XLs provides better entertainment than Zig Zag strip club next door thanks to the school uniform dress code for 'Please Sir'. It's equally entertaining, albeit for different reasons, on a Saturday as the Fred Durst and Marilyn Manson wannabes arrive for the alternative rockers night. The club's a suitably dingy affair with no disco-ball pyrotechnics or rotating dancefloors, and this is definitely a 'scene' place that attracts a regular crowd so don't bother just calling in on the off chance after a night 'round Broad Street. This also means that the majority of the crowd are on the same wavelength, which means that the whole place is usually rocking by the end of the night.

■■ Zanzibar
Hurst Street (0121) 643 4715

Treading the path so crudely and brutally

Take a leaf out of our book

forged by the Ritzy's and Roxy's of the 70s and 80s, the Zanzibar chain of cheesy clubs provides a no-frills weekly piss-up for your average punter. After a hard week on the building site, behind the shop counter, or in front of the VDU, many people, it would seem, want nothing more than to be stuck in a couple of cavernous rooms with about a thousand other equally lashed up lads and lasses dancing to exactly the same records they listen to all week on Radio 1. This one's actually a bit smarter than most and comprises four different rooms including the surreal Polo Club lounge. Even if you think you're the coolest kid on the block sometimes it's quite a laugh to just get hammered and make a tit of yourself, and for that occasion Zanzibar's provides the perfect stage.

■■ Best places for:

Techno & Electronica
Atomic Jam @The Que Club, Statik @ Circo
Jazz Soul & Funk
Sofistifunk @ 52 Degrees North, Liquid Vision @ Libertys
House & Garage
Take your pick: Fuel @ Bonds, Peruvia @ Hidden, Mass @ Bakers, Gods Kitchen @ Code.
Indie
Ramshackle @ The Academy
Hip-Hop, R'n'B & Breaks
Trigger @ Medicine Bar, Hi-Fi @ Circo
World Music
Viva Havana @ Ipanema (Salsa), Shanti @ Medicine Bar (Asian)
Drum'n'Bass
Broken Minds @ Sanctuary
Sixties, Motown, Northern Soul
Soul Kitchen @ The Academy, Big Wednesday @ Snobs
Seventies, Eighties, Disco
Please Sir @ XLs
Pop & Rock
Saturday @Tiger Tiger, Saturday @ Bobby Brown's
Classical & Opera
The Royal Concert Hall
Metal/Alternative
Saturday @ XLs

At itchybirmingham.co.uk you'll find content from some of the biggest names in the country. Here are just a few of them...

Big Daddy: Hip Hop, beats aand culture

Deuce: UK garage

Knowledge: Drum 'n' bass

Straight no Chaser: Jazz and all thing funky

Playlouder.com: Like NME but different

www.rizla.com

…clubsclubsclubsclubsclubsclubsclubsclubsclubsclubs

club listings

For more up-to-date reviews, previews and listings check www.itchybirmingham.co.uk

All listings details are subject to change at short notice, and should therefore be used as a guide only.

Club	Night	Music	Price	Closing	Dress code
MONDAY					
The Academy	Pump (Student)	Chart and indie pop	£3 NUS	2am	None
Circo	Melange	Funky breaks, hip hop	Free	2am	None
Medicine Bar	Dub with difference	Dub	Free	11pm	None
TUESDAY					
Circo	Function	House, garage, hip hop	Free	2am	None
WEDNESDAY					
Snobs	Big Wednesday	Indie, 60s, soul	£3	2am	None
Bobby Brown's	Coup (Student night)	Indie, dance, pop	£3.50 NUS	2am	None
Circo	Cocoa	Latin, salsa	Free	2am	None
Medicine Bar (1st Wed)	Lupa	Breaks and beats	Free	2am	None
Medicine Bar (last Wed)	Maji	Live music/art displays	Free	2am	None
THURSDAY					
Mustard Club	Cheese Up (Student)	Chart/dance	£3 NUS	2am	None
Circo	Education	Funky beats	Free	2am	Casual
Code	Session	House	£6/£5 NUS	4am	Clubwear
Ipanema	Viva Havana	Latin and salsa	£3 after 10pm	2am	Smart casual
Liberty's	Salsa night	Salsa	lessons £4	2am	Super tight trousers and ruffled shirts.
Medicine Bar	Heducation	Breaks and beats	£3 after 10pm	2am	None
Stoodi Bakers	Spin (student)	House		2am	Relaxed
Snobs	Love the life	RnB, funk, soul, hip hop	£4	3am	Make an effort
FRIDAY					
52 Degrees	SofistiFunk	Hip hop, funk, jazz	Free	2am	fashionable.
The Academy	Ramshackle	Indie	£5 / £4 NUS	3am	None
Bakers	Wallop	Hard House	£7/5 + flyer	4am	Glamorous
Bonds	Fuel	House	£6 B4 11. £8 aft	2.30	Cool + smooth
Code	God's Kitchen	Hard House	£10/£9 membs	4am	Clubwear
Circo (1st Fri)	Fire and Theft	House	Free	2am	none
Circo (2nd Fri)	Slakin'	Hip Hop	Free	2am	none
Circo (3rd Fri)	Statik	Electro	Free	2am	none

Roll up

itchy**birmingham** 2002

FRIDAY cont'd

Circo (4th Fri)	Alegro	Funky beats	Free	2am	None
Hush	C.R.E.A.M.	House	£12/£10 membs	7am	Club casual
Hidden	Clique	House, breaks & beats	£8 after/£6 NUS	6am	Club cool
Liberty's		Commercial dance	£4 after 9.30	2am	Casual
Liberty's (last)	Liquid fusion	Jazz, fusion	£5	2am	Smart
Medicine Bar(1st)	Procession	Drum n bass	Free b4 9, £2 aft	2am	None
Medicine Bar(2nd)	Sweat	Jazz, funk	Free b4 9, £2 aft	2am	None
Medicine Bar (3rd)	Subspace	Progressive house	Free b4 9, £2 aft	2am	None
Medicine Bar (4th)	Shaanti	Asian dance	Free b4 9, £2 aft	2am	None
Tiger Tiger	Tiger Tiger	Commercial dance	£5 after 10pm	2am	Smart
The Sanctuary	Broken Minds	Drum & Bass	£5	4am	None
XLs	Please Sir	70s, 80s, 90s	£5	2am	School uniform

SATURDAY

The Academy	Blast	Indie/rock	£5 NUS £6	3am	None
(1st Sat)	Soul Kitchen	60s, 70s, funk, soul	£5/£4 NUS	3am	None
Bonds	Mirrorball	House	£8 B4 11pm £10	2.30am	
Bakers	Mass	Hard House	£7/5 with flyer	4am	Clubwear
Circo	Hi Fi	Funk, hip hop, beats	Free	2am	Cool casual
Code	Babooshka	Garage and house	£12/£10 NUS	4am	Clubwear.
Hidden	Peruvia	vocal house./funk.	£12/£10 B4 11	6am	Club cool.
Hush	The Underground	House	£12/£10 membs	7am	Club casual
Liberty's		Commercial dance	£6 after 9.30	2am	Smart
Medicine Bar (1st)	Earko	Electronica	Free b4 9, £2 aft	2am	None
Medicine Bar (2nd)	Nu Tonik	Breakbeat	Free b4 9, £2 aft	2am	None
Medicine Bar (3rd)	Leftfoot	Dub, deep beats	Free b4 9, £2 aft	2am	None
Medicine Bar (4th)	Trigger	Breaks n beats	Free b4 9, £2 aft	2am	None
Que Club	Atomic Jam	Techno/drum n bass	£10/£8 NUS	6am	None
Tiger Tiger	Tiger Tiger	Dance, chart, motown	£5 after 10pm	2am	Smart
Sanctuary	Sundissential	V. hard house	£10/8 members,	4am	Anything glows.
XLs		Rock, Nu metal	£5	2am	Black is advisable

SUNDAY

Bakers	Republica	House	chirpy'n'cheap		Chicken suits
Circo	Makossa	Relaxed vibe	Free	12.30	None

www.itchybirmingham.co.uk

RIZLA+ It's what you make of it.

gay

No longer the black hole of civilisation en route between Manchester and London, Birmingham is thumping the drum of activity and giving the locals more and more reason not to bugger off to Manchester. There's a new kid on the block in the shape of the DV8 Club which is kicking the old boys into touch.

Bars

Angels Café Bar
127-131 Hurst Street (0121) 244 2626
Bit of a scene leader this one, right in the heart of Brummie gay land attracting a varied pre-clubbing crowd of gay men, lezzies and their straight mates. Food is served until 9pm, by which time the clubbing takeover has insured that the intimate dancefloor is packing them in as a warm up to the night time adventures.
Mon-Thu 2-11pm. Fri-Sat 12-12, Sun 12-11pm

Boots Bar
77 Wrentham Street (0121) 622 1414
If you've been to Amsterdam and done the scene, you'll feel a familiar tug as you walk into Boots. A dress code bar, for aficionados of denim, leather or skin. Covering the full age spectrum, this is a must for those who like to tickle or tackle the under-belly of the gay scene. Beware the music is highly questionable, but hey that's not really why you're there, right?
Mon-Thu 2-11pm, Fri-Sat 12-12, Sun 12-11

Missing
Hurst Street (0121) 622 4256
If John Inman and the cast from Hi-De-Hi were waltzing along the bar this place could-

gay
www.itchybirmingham.co.uk

in association with gay.uk.net

n't get much more camp. With cabaret every night, running the full spectrum of drag artists, live PA's and strippers, you'll be hard pressed to sit and ponder Plato in this bar. But why would you want to? There's also the enchantment of the Alexander restaurant upstairs and the beer garden for topping up your tan in Brummie's answer to the Med.
Mon-Wed 12-11, Thu-Sun 12-12

■■ Partners Bar
27-35 Hurst Street, next to the Hippodrome Theatre (0121) 622 4710
By the time you read this Partners may be no longer, not that they're rolling over into an early grave, no! The place is under new management and is lined up for a major refurb and re-launching under a new name. But don't worry this place is slap bang in the middle of homo-street so you'll have no trouble finding it, as things stand it's a very friendly place, with the ensemble line up of strippers, cabaret artists and a little dancefloor for you to shake your chart happy bits to. It does need a major lick of paint, so keep an eye as this could soon be the place that the Birmingham elite meet.
Mon-Sat 1-11, Sun 2-10.30

■■ The Green Room Café/Bar
Hurst Street – opposite the Hippodrome (0121) 605 4343
Bit of a luvvie hang out this one, very Boho and black polo, so don't expect to see any muscle Mary's comparing pec movements. A healthy blend of gay boys and girls and very popular with the pre-theatre drinking crowd, so get your popcorn ready you never know you might feel tempted to join them. Or stay and check out the food, which is dead tasty but don't drop any on your black jumper will you?
Mon-Sat 1-11, Sun 2-10.30

■■ The Jester
Horsefair, Holloway Circus (0121) 643 0155
A regular old timers pub, claiming to be the oldest in town - I'm happy to believe that. Nonetheless a friendly crowd and drinks promotions make this worth the occasional visit, especially if you've always had a secret yearning for the good ol' days. Drag acts and karaoke keep the locals entertained.
Mon-Sat 1-11, Sun 2-10.30

The Daily Telegraph — Britain's biggest-selling quality daily newspaper

www.itchybirmingham.co.uk

■■ The Fox
17 Lower Essex Street (0121) 622 1210
The girls flock here en masse. This is one of the few places aimed at lesbians in the West Midlands, and you've got to ask why, as there sure as hell are women-a-plenty. There's an open welcome to all women and a vast variety of the female form to weave your way through. Hosts the pre-Fussy Pussy party on the first Friday each month, though leave your cat nip at home.
Mon-Sat 6-11

■■ Clubs

■■ DV8
16 Kent Street (0121) 666 6366
Birmingham's newest gay club and like fresh flesh on any scene, everyone wants a slice. The dancefloor is huge, the décor incredible and the drinks offers evil. At present only open from Thursday to Sunday; Thursday is the camp and cheesy buy-one-get-one-free night, (is that to persuade the punters that they're really not dancing to The Brotherhood Of Man?) On Fridays things get serious in the classic house camp and you can get your best togs on for much of the same on Saturday, with added camp.
Fri-Sun 10-4

■■ Nightingale
Essex House, Kent Street (0121) 622 1718
He's the daddy as the saying goes, and it remains the main contender offering three floors of full on action six nights of the week. Tuesdays is the unofficial student night with pints and mixers at £1.50. The place is always packed with every form of gay man that Birmingham has to offer. The place could definitely do with a major makeover; the wooden flooring must look like a haggard old drag queen in daylight. Still, the strippers, live PAs and weekly drinks offers keep them coming. With DJs on every floor, you can run the whole musical gauntlet from full on frothy handbag to dark and dirty techno. There's also a beer garden, restaurant and lounge.
Mon-Thu 10pm-2am, Fri/Sat 9-3.30am, Sun 9-1am, Fittings Leather Bar 6pm-10.30pm. Wheelchair access.

■■ Subway City
27 Water Street, Old Snow Hill (0121) 233 0310
The only club to give The Nightingale a bit of competition, and they succeed largely in this aim. The music is harder and the vibe cooler, though not physically, so get ready to sweat. The nights are colour coded for those of you who are either illiterate or else find yourself such after the witching hour. The first Saturday of the month is Blue for the full on hard thrust, while on the third Saturday it's Pink.
Mon-Sat 10pm-2am, Sun 10pm-12am.

■■ Birmingham Gay Switchboard
(0121) 622 6589
Help for both lesbians and gays.
7pm - 10pm every night of the year.

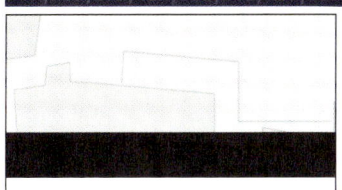

Hair – Men

City Clippers
137 School Rd, Moseley (0121) 444 1088
Mon-Fri 9-6. Sat 8-4
£8

Headman
788 Bristol Rd, Selly Oak (0121) 471 1888
Mon-Wed 10-5.30. Thu-Fri 10-6. Sat 10-5
£5-6

Michaels
451 Brook Lane (0121) 624 6222
Mon-Fri 9-5. Sat 9-3
£5

Hair – Women

Phase 2
691 Bristol Rd South (0121) 475 4329
Mon-Fri 9-5 exc. Thu 9-8. Sat 8.30-5
Cuts from £18.90

Rimski Hair
852 Bristol Rd, Selly Oak (0121) 472 0445
Tue-Sat 9-5.30
£20+

Hair – Unisex

Azura
489 Bristol Rd, Selly Oak (0121) 472 6289
Mon-Sat 9-5.30
Women £10. Men £7

Boo
43 Stephenson St (0121) 632 5949
Get a beer whilst getting your barnet cut.
Mon-Fri 9.45-6. Sat 8-6. £25-35

---

body

www.itchybirmingham.co.uk

body

Eden
11 Ethel Street (0121) 633 3834
Mon-Fri 10-5. Saturday 9-3
Women £28. Men £25

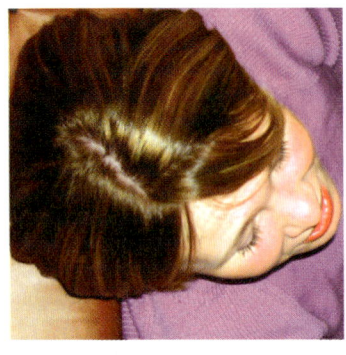

Toni & Guy
Cannon Street (0121) 631 3333
Mon-Fri 9.30-6. Sat 9-3
Women £28-36. Men £23-30

Umberto Gianni
The Waters Edge, Brindleyplace
(0121) 633 0111
Mon-Wed 10-7. Thu-Fri 10-8. Sat 8.30-5
Women £20-35. Men £18-27.50

Tattoo and Piercing

Crafty Jungle
101 Alcester Road (0121) 449 2625
Body piercing specialist.
Piercings from around £6.
Mon-Sat 10-5.30

Graven Images
179 High Street (0121) 753 2389
Tattoos from £15

Mad Ink
Suran Ctre, Coventry Rd (0121) 693 0166
Tattoos from around £10
Mon-Sat 10-5.30 closed Wed, Sun.

Tattooz
819 Stratford Road (0121) 778 3779
Tattoos from around £10
Mon-Sat 10-5.30 (Thu 10-7.30)

Beauty

The Body Shop
New Street (0121) 233 1239
Natural beauty products.
Mon-Sat 9.30-6. Sun 11-5

Clarins Studio
Corporation Street (0121) 212 2336
Facials, waxing, manicures and pedicures.
Mon-Sat 9-6. Sun 11-5

Lush
31 Corporation Street (0121) 643 2700
Handmade smelly stuff for the ladies.
Mon-Fri 9-6. Sat 11-5

Tranquilo Beauty Centre
3rd floor, Guildhall Building, Navigation St
(0121) 687 7717
Top to toe beauty. They can make old turkeys into spring chickens apparently.
Mon-Wed, Fri 10-6. Thu 10-8.30. Sat 10-4

The Daily Telegraph — Britain's biggest-selling quality daily newspaper

■■ Health Clubs

Treat membership prices like buying a used car – whatever price they first offer, tut loudly, sigh outwardly and walk away. There's always special offers, and if you can convince them that you're trying it out before all your mates join, then you'll be quids in.

■■ Curves & Co.
41 Smallbrook Queensway
(0121) 643 8712
Providing entertainment for leary Queensway punters, Curves & Co. overlooks the street with a massive array of treadmills, rowing machines and other CV equipment.
From £3.45 per week

■■ LA Fitness
Unit 5, Temple Row (0121) 632 3950
Well-equipped gymnasium with cardiovascular training facilities, free weights, steam room and jacuzzi.
Mon-Fri 6am-10pm. Sat-Sun 10-6

■■ Living Well Health Club
3 Brunswick Arcade, Brindleyplace
(0121) 633 4645
Gymnasium and aerobics.
Gold membership £49.
Regular membership £39
Mon-Fri 6.30am-10.30pm. Sat-Sun 10-7

■■ Leisure Centres

■■ Aston Villa Sports & Leisure Centre
8 Aston Hall Road (0121) 464 8330
Football pitches, squash courts.
Mon-Sun 10am-11pm

■■ Birmingham Sports Centre
Balsall Heath Road (0121) 464 6060
Large number of sports courts and pitches, plus martial arts lessons and weightlifting facilities.
Mon-Sun 8.40am-10pm

■■ David Lloyd Club
Shady Lane (0121) 325 0700
Well-equipped sports and leisure centre. Tennis, squash, badminton facilities and more.
Mon-Sat 7am-11pm. Sun 8am-10pm

■■ Gillets Sports Centre
998 Bristol Road, Selly Oak
(0121) 415 2300
Fairly small leisure centre with swimming pool and squash courts.
Opening times vary.

www.itchybirmingham.co.uk

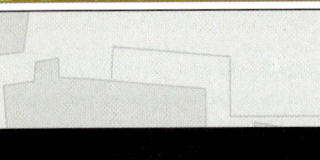

shopping

www.itchybirmingham.co.uk

Markets

Indoor Market
Edgbaston Street (0121) 607 6000
Putting a market indoors seems to somehow miss the point. It's just not the same without the rain, the dirt and the rubbish is it? Nearly a hundred stalls with a wide selection of butchers, grocers, fishmongers and clothing sellers, now housed in this spanking new building. Surely home to some of the cheapest wares in the country.
Mon-Sat 9-5.30

St Martin's Market
Edgbaston Street (0121) 303 0300
Understandably disrupted in recent times but the market usually has a huge number of stalls banging out all kinds of bargains.
Tues, Fri, Sat 9-4.30

Shopping Centres

City Plaza
47 Cannon Street (0121) 633 3969
City Plaza has, in recent times, stood as the undisputed fashion leader of Birmingham shopping centres, but is now under threat from the Mailbox. This of course is good news for us (or at least for those of us with

money to spend) and I don't see the Plaza taking it lying down. There's also a number of cafes to compliment the clothes stores.
Mon-Sat 8.30-6. Sun 10-5

■■ The Fort
20 Fort Parkway, off the M6 between junction 5 and 6.
It proves incredibly easy to infiltrate the Fort, as they provide 2000 free parking spaces and a whole host of clothing, home furnishing, sports, and electrical shops, including Next, Oasis, JD Sports, Dixons, and a WHSmiths. As the shops are all individual units, the Fort can't make the claim to cater for all your shopping needs under one roof, but it can be a lot less hassle than the city centre if you're not looking for anything too specialist.
Mon-Fri 9.30-8 (Thu 9pm) Sat 9.30-7. Sun 11-5pm.

■■ The Mailbox
Suffolk Street Queensway, Royal Mail Street (0121) 643 4080
Whatever your thoughts on shopping centres on the whole it is refreshing to see one with so much more style and identity than the typical purpose-built boxes that you find along the nation's motorways. Well, OK, it is a big box, but it's bright red, striking to look at, and genuinely stylish. Good job too, otherwise all the salubrious and exclusive fashion outlets would look out of place, including DKNY, Hugo Boss, Iceberg, Joop! and Nitya to name but a few. They will also soon be housing Harvey Nichols, which as Leeds knows, means that we're all dead posh in this city, right our kid?
Mon-Sat 10-6pm. Sun 11-5.

■■ The Merry Hill Centre
Brierley Hill, West Midlands (01384) 481 141
This is your archetypal out-of-town Americanised mega-mall. Everything you need for the complete shopping experience under one roof, as long as you don't require any personality or character. On the plus side there's a few independents along with all the high street regulars, and there's plenty of free parking.
Mon-Fri 10-8. Sat 9-7. Sun 11-5.

■■ The Pallasades
New Street (0121) 633 3070
Not great, but it is trying. The area around New Street station is still a pretty ugly part of town, and that has hampered the

www.itchy**birmingham**.co.uk

shopping

Pallasades attempts at achieving a stylish identity. It's pretty standard stuff with a JJB Sports and a Time Computers. Maybe once the redevelopment of the area is finished then the Pallasades might begin to fulfil its potential. In the meantime, listen out for bored security staff whiling away their nights by hurling abuse at pissed-up punters through tannoys on McDonald's ramp, all from the safety of their CCTV enclaves.
Mon-Sat 9-5.30. Thu 9-7. Sun 11-5.

■■ Pavilion Central
38 High Street (0121) 631 4121
Pretty traditional (as in 80s) shopping centre. Hardly overflowing with quirky independent stores but it does have some of the high street favourites, including HMV and Marks and Spencers, and an excellent Waterstone's. A newly renovated food floor looks like it's been the motive for rebranding from Pavilion to Pavilion Central. As opposed to Pavilion North? We don't understand.

■■ Priory Square Shopping Centre
Priory Walk (0121) 236 5303
Slightly bizarre shopping centre, with Argos and Virgin vying for custom with some pretty shonky market trader types. Whatever you're looking for you'll find one here. You might not find a good one, but you'll find one. The best bit is Oasis tucked in and amongst all the chaos – not the clothes store, but a long-standing collection of independent traders housing everything from the weird and wonderful, to the grungy and tasteless.

Nick, 25, Student

Best place for a drink in town?
Gun Barrels, always lively
A student indeed. And for a club?
Jam House has got that something extra
True enough. How about for a restaurant?
All Bar One
I think he misheard. Favourite shop?
Cult Clothing
What's great about Birmingham?
Cheaper than London
And what's not?
It's too spread out

■■ Department Stores

■■ BHS
6-9 New Street (0121) 643 8541
Conservative, sensible clothing that you hated as a kid, but are starting to see the practicality of these days. Go on, admit it.
Mon-Sat 9-6 ('til 8 Thu), Sun 11-5

■■ Marks and Spencer
42 High Street (0121) 643 4511
Going back to basics after its brief and unsuccessful flirtation with designer labels and high fashion.
Mon-Wed 8-6, Thu-Fri 8-7, Sun 11-5

PLAN YOUR RESIGNATION TACTICALLY

■■ Muji
ew Street (0121) 643 1764
panese lifestyle shop. Not as big as your nventional department store, but a lot ore interesting. Clothing, stationery, and omeware. The pyjamas are especially wicked.
Mon-Sat 9-6 ('til 7 Thu), Sun 11-5

■■ Rackhams
Corporation Street (0121) 236 3333
The House of Fraser is a veritably posh house at that. It carries some pretty high-end fashion labels, your obligatory perfume-spraying, home furnishings and multi-media type gubbins. Like Selfridges, only not.
Mon-Sat 9.30-6 ('til 8 Thu), Sun 11-5

■■ Clothing – Unisex

■■ A2
9 Ethel Street (0121) 643 3989
Cool streetwear from brands like Duffer of St George and Evisu.

■■ Breed
Bristol Road, Selly Oak
If you ever want to convince yourself that Selly Oak is crap, for clothes as well as food, then look no further than this shoebox of a shop. Without even the briefest of licks of paint, they opened up this store with some stuff that may appeal to the retro crowd, but with the prices they charge and the lack of variety with it, you'd be better off looking somewhere else for your wardrobe.

■■ Cult Clothing
29/30 Stephenson Street (0121) 643 1051
Good selection of streetwear with an urban skater influence. Racks of t-shirts, combats and cool threads for the kids.

■■ Diesel
8-9 Lower Temple Street (0121) 632 5575
Denim is officially cool again and The Diesel brand has certainly played its part in the revival.

■■ Fire and Ice
The Minories, Temple Court (0121) 236 8545
Rugged outdoor clothing with a touch of street style. Rockport, Berghaus, Quiksilver.

■■ Gap
40 New Street (0121) 633 0644
Like Marks and Spencer's streetwise American cousin, this is mostly pretty simple high street stuff but with a little bit more class.

REMEMBER, LEAVE ON A POSITIVE NOTE.

www.itchy**birmingham**.co.uk

shopping

Grandma takes a Trip
Ethel Street
I remember my Gran having one too many snowballs at Christmas once, and that's a disturbing enough thought. As strange as it sounds, most of the clothing strays on the charitable side of retro, but you'll find the odd hidden gem here.

Nicholls
1 Temple Row (0121) 687 5557
Good quality, but pricey designer gear. Armani, Hugo Boss, DKNY etc.

Yo Yo
7 Ethel Street (0121) 633 3073
Remember, prices may go up as well as down (like trousers). Funky retro gear.

Clothes Men

Acid Test
34 Stephenson Street
(0121) 643 6224
Fairly smart own brand gear. Not particularly psychedelic though.

Autograph
15/17 Ethel Street
(0121) 633 3540
Label hunters should find all the names they're looking for in Autograph. Dries Van Noten, Paul Smith, Vivienne Westwood and other leading names from the fashion scene are all available in what is one of the best menswear shops in Brum.

GS3
Stephenson Street (0121) 643 9292
Small menswear shop that carries essential clothes for 'mod'ern life. Teddy Smith, Fred Perry and Lambretta.

Life
36 Stephenson Street (0121) 633 0792
Small but pretty good menswear shop with some smart designer label gear. Prada Sport, Boss, Armani, Replay.

Limeys
14 Stephenson Street (0121) 643 3227
Pretty decent menswear store with a standard selection of street and smarter clothes.

"WHEN YOU'RE SACKED, YOU CAN WORK FOR ME"

itchy**birmingham** 2002

shopping

■■ Love
Stephenson Street (0121) 643 2624
Mostly own-brand gear from local designer Donovan Love. They'll also cut your hair for you.

■■ MC Man
ty Plaza, Cannon Row (0121) 605 5858
art gents clothing store with a good ection of designer gear.

■■ Original Levis Store
5 Caxton Gate, Corporation Street (0121) 632 6450
The flagging popularity of the cowboy look a few years back, saw Levis lose some of its dominance in the market. They've adapted heir style and range in recent times, and here's no disputing the fact that they're still ig players.

■■ Reiss
32 New Street (0121) 632 6054
Quality, stylish own-brand menswear. Not cheap but certainly not extortionate either.

■ Clothes Women

■■ Christian Lacroix
24-26 Wharfeside Street, The Mailbox (0121) 632 1292

Probably only sells about one dress a year, but that should still be enough to keep them in profit.

■■ Cruise Flannels
14 Lower Temple Street (0121) 633 0529
Cool, modern and spacious shop stocking Prada, Gucci and other similarly exclusive labels.

■■ DKNY
6-12 Wharfeside Street (0121) 600 7200
Fabulous darling. A bit out of my league, but that's a definite recommendation.

■■ Eda
Unit 10 Lower Wharfeside Street, The Mailbox (0121) 632 1220
Fancy own-brand lingerie and underwear. Chuffin' Eda though it ain't cheap.

BEWARE OF THE VOICES. FOR CAREER ADVICE WORTH LISTENING TO, INCLUDING **HELP** WITH **INTERVIEWS**, VISIT **monster.co.uk**

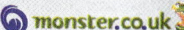

www.itchy**birmingham**.co.uk

RIZLA + WARE
QUALITY CLOTHING

WWW.RIZLA.CO.UK/WARDROBE

shopping

■■ Jigsaw
Cannon Street (0121) 633 9457
Smart modern clothing at reasonable prices.

■■ MC Woman
City Plaza, Cannon Row (0121) 605 4466
Top end gear form Versace, Dolce and Gabbana and Armani. Wallet-raping galore.

■■ Oasis
125 New Street (0121) 643 2770

Designer styles at affordable prices and a fast enough turn-over to ensure you don't end up in the same hipsters as every other girl in your local.

■■ Rhonit Zilkha
21 Wharfeside Street (0121) 632 1299
Exclusive designer fashion boutique in the trendy Mailbox.

■■ Serene Order
Burlington Arcade (0121) 643 5885
Vivienne Westwood and Dexter Wong amongst others in this designer label specialist.

■■ Books

■■ Nostalgia and Comics
14-16 Smallbrook Queensway
(0121) 643 0143
Massive selection of comics, graphic novels, sci-fi books, games and toys.

■■ Waterstone's
Aston Uni, 12 Gosta Green
(0121) 359 3242
24 High Street (0121) 633 4353
128 New Street (0121) 631 4333
The New Street store is probably the flagship, with its lifts, coffee shop and numerous floors, but the library-like high street Waterstone's is equally good in its own more traditional way. All have an excellent selection of books on almost any topic.

■■ WHSmith
29 Union Street (0121) 631 3303
95 High Street, Harborne
(0121) 427 5945
126 Pershore Street (0121) 692 1331
126 Leopold Street (0121) 766 6868
The high street institution that is WHSmith's. Books, magazines, papers and stationery available at most.

itchy sms @
www.itchybirmingham.co.uk

shopping

■■ WHSmith Travel
New Street Station (0121) 643 9235
Grab yourself a book to read while you're waiting for your train to arrive. Make it a thick one. It could be some time.

■■ The Works
137 New Street (0121) 643 3092
8 The Pallasades (0121) 643 2877
Decent selection of books at some bargain prices.

■■ Music

■■ Dance Music Finder
2nd Floor, Smithfield House, Moat Lane
(0121) 622 5885
Helpful staff who'll give you a hand tracking down those essential dance tunes.

■■ Dancefaze Records
105 Market Street, Hednesford
(01543) 87624
OK, it's a bit out of the way, but if you're after the latest trance and hardhouse anthems then you'll find it worth the journey.

■■ Hard to Find Records
10 Upper Gough Street (0121) 687 7773
It's been going for over ten years so they clearly know what they're doing. This vinyl emporium is essential shopping for all would be DJs. Almost all genres of dance are in stock, along with a selection of turntables and DJ kit too. They also provide a catalogue and online ordering service.

■■ HMV
Pavilion Central, 38 High Street
(0121) 643 2177
3 The Pallasades (0121) 633 7447
The HMV in the Pallasades is fairly small but it carries a good selection of the latest rock, pop and dance releases. The Pavilion store is a much more impressive affair with specialist departments for dance, classical, books and videos.

■■ The Jazz and Swing Record Centre
45-46 Loveday Street, Aston
(0121) 359 7399
No we haven't got the new Alien Ant Farm album, you moron.

■■ Jibbering Records
Alcester Road, Moseley (0121) 449 4551
Relaxed record shop specialising in all things phat and phunky. Excellent selection of 70's funk and world music, plus newer offerings.

itchy**birmingham** 2002

WATERSTONE'S BOOKSELLERS
In Birmingham

W

Two great bookstores for all your leisure and academic reads

24-26 High Street
Birmingham B4 7SL
t: 0121 633 4353

128 New Street
Birmingham B2 4DB
t: 0121 631 4333

www.waterstones.co.uk

■■ Reddington Rare Records
Lower Ground Floor, Smithfield House, Digbeth (0121) 622 7050
RRR should be moving to their new premises by the time you read this. Unfortunately they weren't planning a clearance sale before they went. Good selection of second hand records and rarities of most genres from rock, pop, punk and metal.

■■ Swordfish Records
14 Temple Street (0121) 633 4859
Proper alternative to the standard high street megastore, Swordfish has racks of CD and vinyl, mainly from the rock, punk, and indie genres.

■■ Tempest Records
83 Bull Street (0121) 236 9170
Dance music vinyl specialist with a good selection of house and garage. Slightly intimidating for those who don't know their time signatures and their tempos.

■■ Tower Records
5 Corporation Street (0121) 616 2677
Big selection of CDs, videos, books, magazines, and even some vinyl.

■■ Virgin Megastore
98 Corporation Street (0121) 236 2523
Everything you'd expect from a Virgin Megastore. Racks of CDs, videos, DVDs, and books.

www.itchybirmingham.co.uk

WHATEVER TURNS YOU ON   Virgin megastores

shopping

■■ Other Cool Stuff

■■ The Artlounge
Lower Wharfeside Street, The Mailbox
(0121) 632 1471
Contemporary art gallery with some cool stuff for your new city centre apartment.

■■ Globe-Trotter
Unit 37, Wharfeside Street, The Mailbox
(0121) 632 1360
The only way to travel in style. For those who are prepared to spend more on luggage than most of us spend on the actual holiday.

■■ Ideal
175 Corporation Street (0121) 236 3900
The best skateboards and skating hardware, plus a wicked selection of footwear and clothing from labels like Una Bomber, Zero, Vans and loads of others.

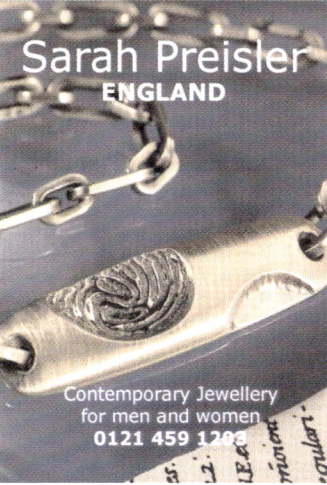

Sarah Preisler
ENGLAND

Contemporary Jewellery
for men and women
0121 459 1203

■■ Legends Boardriders
City Plaza, Cannon Row (0121) 633 0296
Excellent selection of surfing, skating and boarding gear, clothing and footwear. Oxbow, O'Neill, Quiksilver.

■■ Sara Preisler
(0121) 459 1203
Contemporary jewellery for men and women.

■■ Stuff and Co.
5b Ethel Street (0121) 633 8835
Some life-saving ideas for last minute birthday or Christmas presents. All manner of gifts and quirky stuff.

NIGHTMARES ON WAX • COM

www.itchy**birmingham**.co.uk

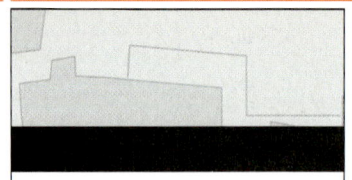

entertainment

entertainment
www.itchybirmingham.co.uk

Entertainment Centres

It appears to be the fashion to spend millions on development in Brum...

Star City has probably made the biggest impact to date, with its Vegas-inspired glitz and lights. Now well into its second year, opinions range from it being an "all in one entertainment extravaganza" (the PR office) to "Star City, aka Scab city, a soulless Americanised heap of junk in a duff part of town" (snobbish Arcadian bar-goer). Neither's true. It's fair to say that it's lacking in character, with all the average chain restaurants putting in a fake grinned, microwaved appearance. And it's never going to be the centre of high culture. And it's a veritable pain in the arse to get to. But ignoring all that, if you want to go the cinema, 30 screens is always going to help, and if you like bowling – well, why go anywhere else? As such, the place is usually heaving, so who cares what anyone else thinks?
Watson Road, Nechells, Just off M6 Jct 6
08708 44 66 00

The Five Ways Leisure Park is a bit of an enigma. You expect some enclosed entertainment complex, and yet it's a few enter-

itchy**birmingham** 2002

tainment venues spread across one of the busiest roundabouts in the city. Tiger Tiger, and now Brooklyn Vodka Bar and a cinema to name but a few. Opening in Summer 2002, just to really piss them off, is a rival entertainment complex on the other side of the island called **Broadway Plaza**, housing – yes, yet another cinema, Esporta healthclub and shag me ragged if it's not another bowling alley, sorry Bowlplex. Time will tell who wins... Bothered?

And finally, there's **Millennium Point**. Six football pitches of entertainment – well, actually only two attractions, but given that they cost £114 million they must be expecting a fair few visitors. The IMAX is impressive, and given the amount of money it costs, the new Thinktank should give Brum the science museum it deserves, ie be interesting, not the dusty old yawn-inspiring atom sculptures and clipboard dreariness of your old school visits.
Millennium Point, Curzon Street
0800 48 2000

Cinemas

IMAX
Millennium Point (0121) 464 1977
With each frame of film being 10 times the size of a normal cinema, it takes millions and millions of spondoolicks to develop even the simplest of flicks. That means that the infamous documentaries on the plains of Serengeti will doubtlessly make an appearance, alongside classics about the Arctic exploration. But never fear – no matter how interested you aren't in the migration of antelope, watching a film on IMAX is well and truly spectacular, so you've got to go at least once.

Mac (Midlands Art Centre)
Cannon Hill Park (0121) 440 8838
Ranging from the famous to the worthy, they give the latest blockbusters a miss, but they often have true classics and a few moustache-twiddling art-house films. Also see art galleries.

Odeon Cinema
New Street (0870) 505 0007
Train delayed again? You might just be able to sneak in a Star Wars triple-header in this cinema that's just a quick dash from the station.
£4.50 adults, £3.50 concs.

Showcase Cinema
Kingsbury Road, Erdington
(0121) 382 9779. Booking (0121) 382 4749
Prices from £4

...EVERYONE WELCOME

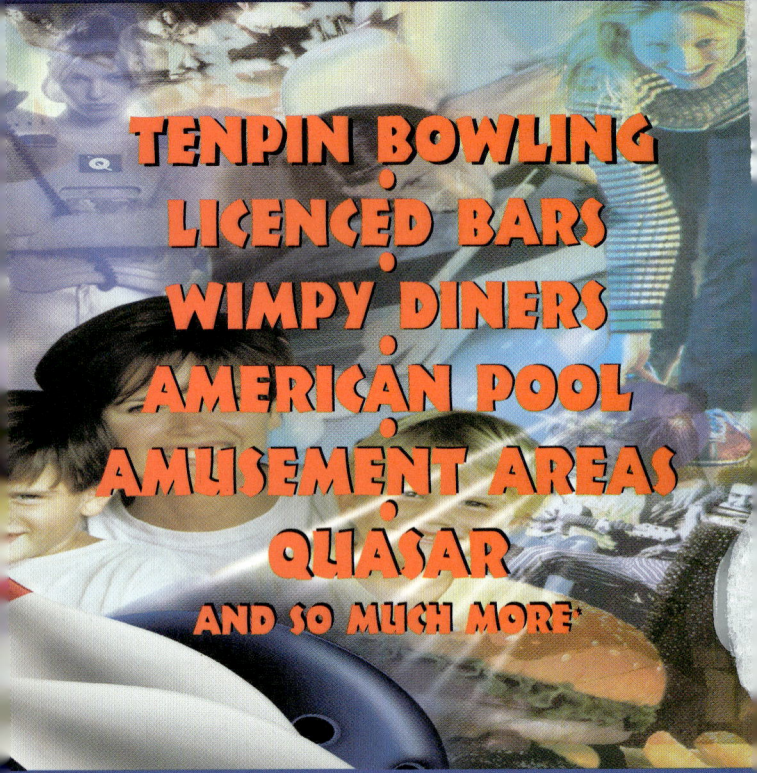

**TENPIN BOWLING
LICENCED BARS
WIMPY DINERS
AMERICAN POOL
AMUSEMENT AREAS
QUASAR
AND SO MUCH MORE***

**TO FIND YOUR NEAREST MEGABOWL VISIT OUR WEBSITE
OR CALL TALKING PAGES FREE ON 0800 600 900**

*Facilities vary at each Megabowl

MEGABOWL

www.megabowl.co.uk

entertainment

■■ UGC
Arcadian Centre, Hurst St (0870) 155 5177
Plenty of restaurants around if you want to make an evening of it.
£5 adults, £3.50 concs.

■■ UGC
Five Ways Leisure Park, Broad Street (0870) 907 0723
Plenty of bars around if you want to make a mess of it in this swanky cinema complex.
£5 adults, £3.50 concs.

■■ Warner Village
Star City, Junction 6 M6
In a galaxy far far away. Well a few stops down the M6 anyhow. With 30 screens, yes 30, it's not only one of the biggest in Europe (it was when we went to print, but we're covering ourselves), it means that if you can't find something worth seeing here then you're obviously a twat.
£5.50 adults, £4 concs.

■■ Bowling

■■ Hollywood Bowl
Great Park, Park Way (0121) 453 0333
Open 10am-11pm
£2.50 Mon-Fri before 6. £3.75 per frame at all other times.

■■ Megabowl
Pershore Street (0121) 666 7525
Open 12pm-11.30pm
Last games commence at 10pm
£4.25 first frame. £3.75 additional games.

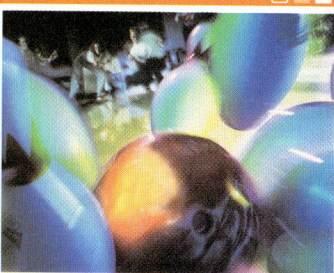

■■ Star City Megabowl
Watson Road, Nechells (0121) 327 8483
Luminous balls, disco lights and throwing shapes. Such is Star City's 22-lane bowling extravaganza at night-time. It doesn't get much bigger than this, and better, in a bizarre stripey-shoed kind of way.
Open 10am-12.30am
£3.75 per game.

■■ Theatres

■■ Alexandra Theatre
Station Street (0121) 643 5536 Box Office (0870) 607 7544
Handily placed for rail travellers, this theatre may not have the most illustrious of surroundings but it does stage many of the top shows straight from the West End.

■■ Birmingham Hippodrome
Hurst Street (0870) 730 5555
Now housed in its spanking new multi-million pound building, the Hippodrome looks set to confirm itself as the numero uno theatrical venue in Brum.

The Daily Telegraph — Britain's biggest-selling quality daily newspaper

www.itchybirmingham.co.uk

entertainment

■■ Birmingham Repertory Theatre
**Centenary Square, Broad Street
(0121) 245 2000
Box Office (0121) 236 4455**
Well respected repertory theatre that stages a wide variety of dramatic productions using a wealth of local talent.

■■ Royal Shakespeare Company
**Waterside, Stratford-upon-Avon
(0178) 929 6655
Box Office (0178)940 3403**
Worth travelling out to for fans of the bard.

■■ Galleries and Museums

■■ Barber Institute of Fine Arts
**The University of Birmingham,
Edgbaston (0121) 414 7333**
An impressive collection of paintings and sculpture from some of the most important names in art history. Modern art pieces accompany works by the old master to divide opinion and stimulate 'My four year old grandson could do better than that' type debate.
Open 10-5 Mon-Sat. 2-7 Sun
Free admission

■■ Birmingham Museum and Art Gallery/Gas Hall
Chamberlain Square (0121) 303 2834
The world's largest permanent collection of Pre-Raphaelite art is housed in this impressive Victorian building. The new adjoining Gas Hall Exhibition Gallery houses temporary shows of all styles.
Open 10-5 Mon-Sat (except Fri 10.30-5)
12.30-5 Sun

■■ Ikon Gallery
1 Oozells Square, Brindleyplace

A suitably cool location for Birmingham's most progressive and forward thinking art space. Good-sized, two-floored gallery playing host to regularly updated exhibits of modern and multi media art. If you're finding some of it too conceptually challenging, have a beer or two in the excellent café and it'll all start to make sense.
Open 11-6 Tues-Sun
Admission: voluntary contribution (don't be a tight git, they've got poor artists to fund)

YOU'RE IN AN INTERVIEW

▪▪ Midlands Art Centre
Cannon Hill Park (0121) 440 4221

The Mac as it is known, is an all-purpose arts and culture centre based in Cannon Hill Park. It's the throbbing heart of art in Brum, with a range of everything - there's a theatre and cinema auditorium, regular art and crafts displays and loads of classes and workshops for the public to join in with. There's even a café and bookshop here too so it's an ideal place for culture vultures to while away the hours.
Open 9-11pm Mon-Sun

▪▪ Museum of the Jewellery Quarter
75-79 Vyse Street, Hockley
(0121) 554 3598

Most locals might consider the Balti mile in Sparkbrook to be the jewel in Birmingham's crown but this museum charts the history of a longer-standing craft. A working museum illustrating the skills and craftsmanship of the traditional jewellery makers that were, and are still, based in this part of the city.
Open 10-4 Mon-Fri. 11-5 Sat
Admission: adults £2.50 concessions £2, family ticket (2 adults 3 children) £6.50

▪▪ NEC
M42 Junction 6 (0121) 767 3888

Massive all-purpose exhibition centre and music venue. Hosts various events throughout the year, most notably Crufts and the Motor Show. There are plenty of other events for those neither interested in cars nor corgi's.

Mike, 23, Web Designer

When you're not playing with your java beans, where's the best place for a drink?
Medicine Bar always hits the spot
How about for a club?
The Sanctuary has a lot of cracking nights
And for a fancy meal?
Kebabland
Fancy indeed. How about your favourite shop?
Diesel's always good
What's good about Brum?
It is trying
And what's bad about it?
Not hard enough.

▪▪ The New Art Gallery Walsall
Gallery Square, Walsall (01922) 654400

Walsall perhaps isn't a noted cultural hot bed, (in fact, not to put too fine a point on it - it's a bit of a shit hole) but this twenty million pound venture is attempting to challenge that image. Despite containing many works from 20th Century artists such as Van Gogh and Monet it may be the building itself that proves the biggest draw. It's a feat of engineering and has been nominated for a series of architectural awards, the likes of which Walsall could previously only dream.

DON'T GET INTIMIDATED BY THEIR EYE CONTACT

www.itchybirmingham.co.uk

entertainment

■■ Waterhall Gallery
Chamberlain Square (0121) 303 2834
Impressive new gallery which specialises in modern art.

■■ Days out and Attractions

■■ Alton Towers
Stoke-on-Trent (0870) 520 4060
Anyone who grew up anywhere around the Midlands will have fond memories of school trips to Alton Towers. The Viking ship might seem a lot smaller these days but this is still one of the top theme parks in the country. Alton Towers also acts as an exemplary demonstration for visiting French school children of the mystifying ancient English tradition of forming an orderly queue. Watch and learn.
Open April-Oct
Admission: Adults £17-23 children £14-19 depending on the dates.

■■ Black Country Museum
Tipton Road, Dudley (0121) 520 8054
There's more to the Black Country than the folk who call Toy'R'Us Toys'Am'We. Back in the 1800s, huge industrial work made this area black with pollution in the daytime and red at night. The air's cleared, and keeping the spirit of the area alive is the museum. A lot of it is educational – and so full of morose school kids, living in fear for the test at the end of the day. But it's interesting enough for the adults, and the Dudley Canal Tunnel, leading out into spectacular caverns is a definite must.
Open 10-5pm – 7 days
(Nov-Feb, Wed-Sun 10-4pm)
Admission: adults £7.95, children £4.75
OAPs £6.95, family £21.50 (2 adults, 3 kids)

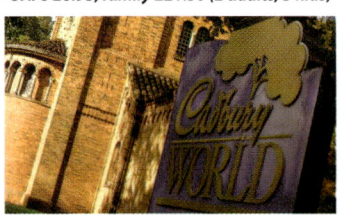

■■ Cadbury World
Linden Road, Bourneville
(0121) 451 4159
No everlasting gob-stoppers, no golden eggs or lickable wallpaper. Just pure unadulterated chocolate, and Cadabra, the most surreal 'ride' since Willy Wonka gave Augustus Gloop a go on his special chocolate expressway. See how it's made, then gorge yourself sick on the stuff from the discount shop.
Admission: adults £8.25, children £6.25,
family ticket (2 adults, 2 children) £24.25

"OI, WHAT ARE YOU LOT STARING AT!?"

104   itchy**birmingham** 2002

entertainment

■■ Drayton Manor Family Theme Park
Tamworth, Staffs (0121) 451 4180

Not exactly Disney World but it's a decent theme park with enough rides and rollercoasters to keep the kids happy. There's also a great big zoo to get back to your roots.
Admission: adults £15, children £11, OAPs/disabled £6.50.

■■ Lickey Hills
Visitor's Centre, Warren Lane, Barnt Green (0121) 447 7106

Ugh, I can't move. My head's bleeding internally, my guts feel rotten and I reckon a day loafing in front of the tele should cure it. No – honestly, take our word for it, and get off your arse and go to the Lickey Hills. It's rare to find this kind of countryside 15 mins from the town centre, and an hour wandering around here will sort out the most chronic of hangovers guaranteed. Or your money back.
Admission free.

■■ National Sea Life Centre
The Water's Edge, Brindleyplace (0121) 633 4700

Not to be confused with the National Pond Life Centre, which is a personal shrine to all my ex-girlfriends, this is a centre dedicated to the wonders of the marine kingdom. As Birmingham is possibly the furthest city from the sea in Britain it was strategically selected to house the National Sea Life Centre in order to scupper any plans that the assorted aquatic animals may be harbouring of making a break for freedom. It's pretty good though.
Open 10-6pm (last admission 4pm)
Admission: £8 adults, £5.95 concessions.

■■ The Shakespeare Houses
The Shakespeare Centre, Henley Street, Stratford-upon-Avon (01788) 920 4016

Do you reckon we could charge £12 for someone to look round the itchy house? 5 Tudor houses all associated with the Bard, allowing you an insight into the world of the most famous playwright and poet of all time.
Admission £12 adults, £6 children

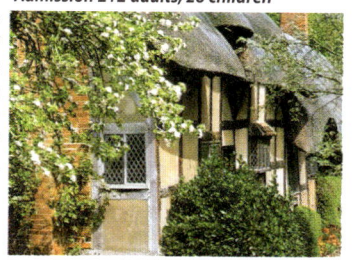

■■ West Midlands Safari and Leisure Park
Spring Grove, Bewdley, Worcestershire (01299) 402 114

Has one of your mates been annoying you showing off their new motor. A bit flash is it? Why not suggest they take everyone out for a spin? Let's go to the West Midlands Safari Park perhaps. Now sit back, relax, and watch as said friend squirms in horror as their new

BEWARE OF THE VOICES. FOR CAREER ADVICE WORTH LISTENING TO, INCLUDING HELP WITH INTERVIEWS, VISIT monster.co.uk

www.itchybirmingham.co.uk

set of wheels is systematically dismantled by a posse of rude-boy baboons. Plenty of theme park rides too, like a baby version of Alton Towers.
Admission: £5.95 (safari park)
£7 (inc rides).

Live Music

Birmingham Academy
Dale End (0121) 262 3000
Impressive from the outside it is not, but who gives a toss when there's the finest live music in Brum inside. Just the right size to house the established and up-and-coming bands, who either aren't quite big enough, or simply don't want to embark on impersonal arena tours.

The Jam House
3 St Pauls Square (0121) 200 3030

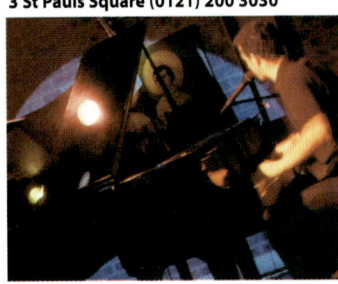

This place belongs to Jools Holland so the predominantly rhythm and blues acts have a high standard to maintain, which they usually do.

NEC
M42 Junction 6 (0121) 767 3888
Enormous all-seater concert venue that catches almost all the bands on national arena tours.

NIA
King Edward Road (0121) 644 6011
Right off Broad Street, like a slightly smaller brother to the NEC, this still impressive venue often plays host to concerts from acts who aren't quite at the stage to fill the largest venues, but are too popular for most gig venues.

Ronnie Scotts
Broad Street (0121) 643 4525
Regular appearances from some of the worlds top names in jazz and blues.

Symphony Hall
Broad Street (0121) 200 2000
Box Office (0121) 780 3333
Looks like a proper classical concert hall should look. Grand, imposing and impressive, it sounds as good as it looks too. Regular performances of the classics from

the Birmingham Symphony Orchestra plus appearances from touring musicians and orchestras.

Comedy

Glee Club
The Arcadian Centre, Hurst Street
0870 241 5063
One of the best UK comedy venues, attracting the cream of the comedy circuit.
Tickets £5-£12.50

Kill For A Seat
Gosta Green, Holt Street, Gosta Green
07939 078865
Not as well known, but still arse crackingly funny. Check www.itchybirmingham.co.uk for listings.
Thursdays, show starts 9pm, £4 admission

Sports and Leisure

Ackers Trust
Golden Hillock Road, Small Heath
(0121) 772 5111
Take a deep breath, and spanning across 70 acres, you can indulge in skiing, snowboarding, climbing, bridgering (ask them), ropes course, canoeing, kayaking, bellboating, archery, 4-wheel drive courses, narrow boat hire and best of all, those management training courses when they make senior management bark like dogs in the name of team spirit.
Open April-October, 10-9 in the week, 'til 6 on the weekend

Tamworth Snow Dome
Leisure Island, River Drive, Tamworth
(0182) 767 905
Full of snow, lots of it, and rad surf dudes careering down the slopes. Beats dry-skiing hands down, and though it's not Val D'Isere, we're not in France.
£21 ph weekends/peak (after 6.30pm)
£17 other times.
Mon-Sun 9am-11pm

Birmingham Bullets (Basketball)
I.C.C Broad Street (0121) 246 6022
Basketball is a high thrills, high skills sport, and these guys are some of the best in the business. If that sounds like I'm being overly complimentary it's because I've seen the size of them.
Tickets start from £8 adults, £5 kids

Aston Villa Football Club
Villa Park (0121) 327 2299
The summer of 2001 saw a remarkable amount of comings and goings at Villa Park, but at the time of going to press manager John Gregory hasn't been one of them.

www.itchy**birmingham**.co.uk

entertainment

Southgate, James, Joachim and half the backroom staff went, and in came Schmeichel, Hadji, Kachloul and Mellberg. The ongoing problems with Villa seem to be routed in a lack of team spirit and unity, and replacing half the English players in the squad with foreign talent is a risky way of trying to remedy the problem. The fans, understandably, are not prepared to settle for being one of the Premiership's second tier, and if the shortcomings are not redressed soon the gap between the Villans and the Premiership elite may become insurmountable. However, if the undeniable talent at the Villa can be harnessed, there is potential to push for the European spot that would help re-establish them as one of the big clubs.
Tickets from £15 (£5 concs.)

■■ Birmingham City
St Andrews, St Andrews Road
(0121) 772 0101
By the end of the 2001-2002 season I fully expect Trevor Francis to either be looking forward to a new season in the Premiership, or looking for a new job at the dole office. Recent history would suggest it's more likely to be the latter, but the Blues should be making a strong push again. Francis, as well as the City faithful, will be desperate for an automatic spot to avoid the seemingly annual heartbreak of the play-offs. The Gold brothers now seem reluctant to throw many more millions at the quest for the holy grail of the Premiership, so don't expect masses of transfer activity this term.
Tickets from £17 (£9 concs.)

■■ Coventry City
Highfield Road, King Richard Street
(024) 7623 4000
The Sky Blues finally lost their top-flight status in 2001 and it was quickly followed by the loss of some of their star players. However the signings of Julian Joachim and Lee Hughes from a couple of their West Midlands neighbours signalled their intent to return to the Premiership. There is still some Premiership quality in the squad and Coventry should be serious contenders to make a quick return to the big time.
Tickets from £15 (£6 concs.)

■■ Walsall
Bescot Stadium, Bescot Crescent, Walsall (01922) 622 791

The West Midlands most successful club of recent years. That might sound like a bold statement but in terms of resources Ray Greardon's achievements of steering the Saddlers to the First Division on two occasions comfortably surpasses Villa's ongoing Premiership obscurity or the Blues, Baggies, and Wolves cumulative failed attempts to achieve top division status. Even if another relegation is imminent, (and I hope it isn't) these are heady times for the Walsall fans to enjoy. With a bit of luck Walsall should have first division status even when this book nears the end of its shelf life.

Tickets from £10 (£8 concs.)

■■ West Bromwich Albion
The Hawthorns, Halford Lane (0121) 525 8888

Making footballing predictions that you have to stand by for 12 months is a risky business that will inevitably leave you with egg on your face. Even taking this into account I'm getting off the fence to predict tough times ahead for the Baggies. I hope I'm wrong, but I suspect that the hopes of returning to the big-time were sold to Coventry. Gary Megson may have created a rod for his own back with the over-achievement he managed in the 2000-2001 season and the expectation of the fans could be hard to live up to. A man that will also be expected to shoulder a large burden of responsibility will be striker Jason Roberts, but how he'll fare now that his prolific partnership with the industrious Lee Hughes has been broken remains to be seen. I'm laying down the gauntlet now, and would be happy to be proved wrong, but it's mid-table at best.

Tickets from £14 (£8 concs.)

■■ Wolverhampton Wanderers
Molineux, Waterloo Road (0121) 655 000

Wolverhampton Wanderer's recent history has proved that in these times of megabucks management can still be more important than millions. The Wolves have had plenty of the latter, but the management of the funds has left a lot to be desired. Consequently, in these now leaner financial times, the prospects of a return to the top flight seem undiminished due to the fans faith in the stewardship of Dave Jones. There are still financial resources at the club, but it's unlikely to be thrown around in such a cavalier fashion as was afforded to previous managers. A year is a long time in football, and Mr Jones could be another managerial casualty by the time you read this, but I'd be surprised. Definitely play-offs and real automatic promotion potential.

Tickets start from £9 (£6 concs.)

■■ Casinos

■■ Birmingham International Casino
Hill Street (0121) 643 1777
Sun-Fri 2pm-6am. Sat 2pm-4am

entertainment

■■ Grosvenor Casino
Broad Street (0121) 631 2414
With swanky bar attached (see bar section)

■■ The Midland Wheel Casino
Norfolk Road, Edgbaston
(0121) 454 3725
Sun-Fri 2pm-5am. Sat 2pm-4am

■■ Strip Clubs

■■ Expose Lap Dancing Club
Fletchers Walk, Paradise Place
(0121) 236 5701
For £10 they take their kit off, for £20 they'll keep the bag on their head.
Mon-Sat 8pm-3am
Admission: £9 before 9pm £10 after.

■■ Legs 11
30 Ladywell Walk (0121) 666 7004
Still, after all these years, competition coming and going, a few venue moves and turbulent times, Legs 11 remains the premier lap-dancing club in Brum. Stick that in your G-string and smoke it.
Mon-Fri 2pm-2am. Sat 7pm-2am.
Admission £10

■■ Spearmint Rhino's
64 Hagley Road, Edgbaston
(0121) 455 7675
The supposedly more salubrious, extravagant and classy American chain of Spearmint Rhino's brings all the best in American lap-dancing entertainment to Brum. Except we've already been doing it here for years. And we've got tons of strip clubs. And I'd hazard a guess that we don't need any more.
Mon-Wed 11am-2am, Thu-Sat 11am-3am, Sun 12pm-12am
Admission £10

■■ Zig Zag
Auchinleck Square, Five Ways
(0121) 673 6743
Mon-Sat 10-3
£10 admission, £5 per dance.

■■ Snooker and Pool

■■ Majestic Snooker club
Station Street (0121) 632 6499

■■ Riley's
Essex Street (0121) 666 6811
Open 24 Hours.
Membership £5. Tables £4 p/h

Have you discovered the G-spot?

Music satisfaction at 102·2

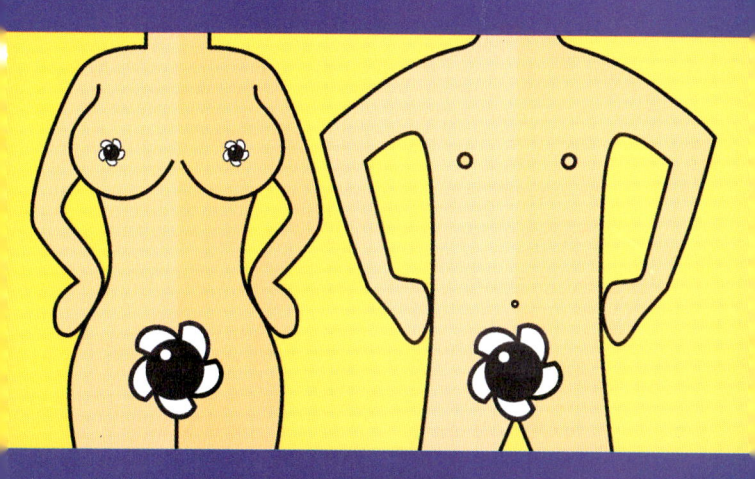

Tune in

Galaxy 102·2

THE NEW MIX FOR BIRMINGHAM

www.galaxy1022.co.uk

itchy cities...

www.itchybirmingham.co.uk

entertainment

■■ Snowhill Snooker Centre
Weaman Street (0121) 233 3953
Open 24 Hours.
£2.80 per hour before 5pm, £3.40 after.

■■ Paintball

■■ National Paintball Fields
Bassetts Pole (0121) 327 3961
Take out your boss, friends or partner. Literally.
£39.50 full day including 600 paintballs and lunch.
11am-dusk.

■■ Karting

■■ Birmingham Wheels Karting Centre
1 Adderley Rd Sth, Saltley (0121) 327 7617
Vrooooooooooooooooooooooooom.
£20 for 30 mins.

■■ Golf – Municipal Courses

■■ Cocks Moors Woods
Alcester Road South, Kings Heath (0121) 464 3584
A lad from my old school once took a Golf GTI and tore up the golf course, handbraking the motor all over the show. They've since patched it up and locked him up.
18 holes £9.50 Mon-Fri, £11 Sat-Sun.

■■ Harborne Church Farm Golf Course
Vicarage Road, Harborne
No Golf GTIs here. Just little carty things.
(0121) 743 9821
18 holes £8.50 Mon-Fri, £10 Fri-Sat.

■■ Hatchford Brook
Coventry Road, Sheldon (0121) 743 9821
18 holes £8.50 Mon-Fri, £10 Fri-Sat.

■■ Hilltop
Park Lane, Handsworth (0121) 554 4463
Surely not practical for a golf course.
18 holes £9.50 Mon-Fri, £11 Fri-Sat.

■■ Golf – Private Courses

■■ The Belfry
The De Vere Belfry, Wishaw, North Warwickshire (01675) 470 033
One of the top courses in the country, as exemplified by its recent status as a Ryder Cup venue. 3 courses, all too tough for shankers like me.

■■ Stonebridge Golf Centre
Somers Road, Meriden, Coventry (01676) 522 442
Pay as you play private golf course.

■■ Greyhound Racing

■■ Perry Barr Greyhound Stadium
Aldridge Road, Perry Barr (0121) 356 2324
Watch Santa's Little Helper go hell for leather chasing a bit of fluff in a circle.
Racing Tues, Thu, Fri, Sat. 6-12
Entry £3.

■■ Hall Green Stadium
York Road (0121) 777 1181
Racing until 10.40. Tue, Fri (from 7.35), Sat (from 7.15)
Entry £5 upstairs, £4 downstairs.

www.itchy**birmingham**.co.uk

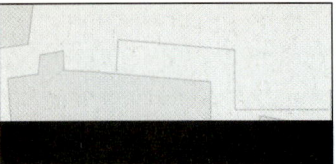

Butties 'n' Baps

Mr Egg
22 Hurst Street (0121) 622 4344
Curiously titled fry-up and butty shop that provides an alternative to all the nearby Chinese restaurants and fancy bars. Opens very late at the weekends as well.
Mon-Thur 8am-6pm. Fri-Sat 8am-4am. Sun 8am-4pm

Chinese

Ivyhouse
213 Monument Road (0121) 454 4215
Closes 11.45

Ling Tung
98 Stechford Road (0121) 783 3785
Closes 11.30

Mr Yeung Chinese Takeaway
Unit 2, Kotwell House, Ladywell Walk (0121) 622 3909
Closes 11.30

Fish and Chips

Bill's Fish Bar
39 Smallbrook Queensway (0121) 643 2322
Closes 11

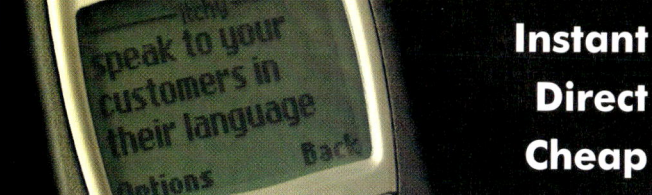

Oi...Venue Managers
It takes 5 minutes to contact all your customers

Instant Direct Cheap

We'll help you build a database of your customers, and give you a simple to use tool to send text messages – it takes no longer than five minutes to send a text to as many people as you wish.

It's cheap (£9 for 100 messages, less for more) and far simpler than designing, printing and distributing flyers. Plus, you know that it will be seen (and by who) and we won't pass on your customers details to anyone else.

For more information call us on **0113 246 0440**, or e-mail **venuemail@itchymedia.co.uk**

Digbeth Fish Bar
90 Digbeth (0121) 616 1085
Closes 12

Indian

Dewan Tandoori
216 St Vincent's St West (0121) 456 4972
Closes 11.30

Star Tandoori
212 Monument Road (0121) 455 6618
Closes 12

Pizza

Caspian Pizza
23 Smallbrook Queensway
(0121) 643 7882
Closes 2am

Christofs
8 Commercial Street (0121) 633 4264
Closes 2am

Burgers and Kebabs

Shahram Kebab House
23 Smallbrook Queensway
(0121) 643 6663
Closes 2am

www.itchy**birmingham**.co.uk

laters

www.itchybirmingham.co.uk

Are you a real wild child or just a weekend warrior? This is where we sort the hardcore from the halfwits.

Late night drinking

There's been an explosion of late night drinking dens in the last four of five years and Brum has now got to be as good as any city outside of the capital for after 11 alcohol consumption. **Circo** was possibly the first to open 'til 2am but now there's plenty of options including **Ipanema** and **Brooklyn** along Broad Street, and most of the bars in the Arcadian like **52 Degrees** and **Sobar**. Most of these places, and plenty of others, are also open 'til half past midnight on a Sunday. So if you're not completely shagged by then and not entirely conscientious about getting to work on Monday morning there's no better way to end the weekend.

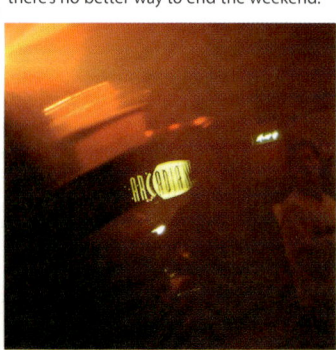

Cigarettes at 4am

Holloway Head service station in the city centre is open 24 hours and should satisfy your late night craving for nicotine/ munchies/milkshake/pornography.

Food now

Mr Egg on Hurst Street will sort you out for a bacon butty at 4am, but if you're feeling a little more exotic then try **Caspian** around the corner on Smallbrook Queensway and they'll source you a greasy doner kebab if you get there for about 2am. Of course there's also plenty of places around the balti triangle that keep going well into the night and cater for the post pub crowd.

Nice food now

It might be midnight but that doesn't mean you have to settle for a supper that flies in the face of all existing health and hygiene conventions. The **Chung Ying Garden** on Thorpe Street in Chinatown is open 'til 12am and is as good a feed as you'll find anywhere in the city anytime. If that's still not giving you enough time to digest your lunch then the **Xaymaca Experience** offers you another hour of decent dining.

Andy, 24, Mac operator

Thirsty work?
I'm always ready for a pint at the Varsity
Club?
Snobs
Best place for a byte?
Kebabland
Where do you pick up your designer gear?
Life
So what's mega about Brum?
The people
And what gives you a floppy?
The Scientologists

top 5 for... Late drinking

1. 52 Degrees (2am)
2. Ronnie Scotts (2am)
3. Sobar (2am)
4. Tiger Tiger (2am)
5. Walkabout (2am)

Post club action

There's only one real option for the hardened clubber looking to keep the night alive: **The Hush**. It doesn't even open its doors until 2am and then pushes through 'til 7am every Friday and Saturday night.

Still not tired?

It's starting to get light but your train's still not due for an hour. Well **Riley's** snooker club on Essex Street never shuts its door.

www.itchybirmingham.co.uk

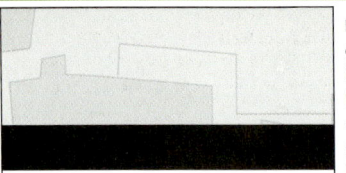

accommodation

www.itchybirmingham.co.uk

Prices given are the cheapest rates that they gave for one person per night and doesn't include breakfast (except B&Bs, obviously). Mind you, that's only a start – speak to the right person on a late booking and you can get better rates if you ask nicely (rather than barter – this never seems to work). On the flip side, they'll bill your ass when it comes to Xmas, so always ring ahead. Also bear in mind that some of these places such as the Days Inn are priced by the room, so it's the same price for a double or a single. Get coupling. We've given the briefest of selections here too. Well, it's not a bloody accommodation guide is it? If you're a bit peeved that this isn't enough, call **Brum's accommodation hotline** on **(0121) 780 4321** and they'll sort you out.

Luxury

Birmingham Marriott
12 Hagley Road, Five Ways
(0121) 452 1144
Edwardian hotel with two fine restaurants.
Single room: £119.

The Burlington Hotel
6 Burlington Arcade, 126 New Street
(0121) 643 9191
Arguably the best hotel in town.
Single room: £135 Mon-Thu. £70 Fri-Sun.

accommodation

■■ Copthorne Hotel
Paradise Circus (0121) 200 2727
Incorporates a purpose built conference and events centre.
Single room: £99 Mon-Thu. £50 Fri-Sun.

■■ Crowne Plaza
Central Square (0121) 224 5053
Swimming pool, leisure facilities and conference rooms.
Double room: £139

■■ Novotel
70 Broad Street (0121) 643 4940
Large 3 star hotel.
Single room: £105

■■ Medium

■■ Chamberlain Tower Hotel
Broad Street (0121) 626 0626
2 star hotel with 250 rooms.
Single room: £55 Mon-Thu. £35 Fri-Sun.

■■ Days Inn
160 Wharfside Street, The Mailbox (0121) 643 9344
Canalside location.
Single room: £55 Mon-Thu. £49.50 Fri-Sun.

■■ Ibis
Ladywell Walk (0121) 622 6010
In the heart of Chinatown.
Single room: £35-55 (dependant on time of year).

■■ Budget

Hagley Rd is full of accommodation, from a selection of reasonable hotels to B&Bs, so if worst comes to the worst, head into this part of town and get door knocking.

■■ The Briar Rose
25 Bennetts Hill (0121) 634 8100
Centrally located hotel incorporating JD Wetherspoons pub, making it our budget hotel of choice.
Single room: £45 Mon-Thurs. £40 Fri-Sun.

■■ Premier Lodge
80 Broad Street (0121) 633 0144
Single room: £46 all week.

■■ Campanile Hotel
Chester Street, Aston (0121) 359 3330
Single room: £41.95 all week.

■■ Bed and Breakfast

■■ Belmont Hotel
419 Hagley Road (0121) 429 1663
Single room: £19

■■ Chard House
289 Mackadown Lane (0121) 785 2145
Single room: £25

From	Subject
itchycity.co.uk	Weekend offers to your inbox

www.itchy**birmingham**.co.uk

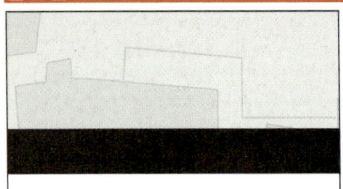

Air Travel

Birmingham International Airport
A45, signposted from M40 and M6
Flight enquiries and information
(0121) 767 7798/9
Car parking (0121) 767 7831
Car parking (long) 0800 128128

Local Bus and Rail

Centro are the unlucky people who've got the job of structuring Birmingham's public transport systems. With all the redevelopment work in and around the city centre at present there is the inevitable disruption to services, but it should all be worth it. Try Centro for all public transport in Brum open 7.30am-10.30pm every day apart from Christmas Day. Yes, even New Year's Day, some poor muppet...
Centro hotline ....(0121) 200 2700

Coach Travel

Digbeth Coach Station
The notoriously grim Digbeth station looks rank whatever they do to it, but bear in mind this whole area's being redeveloped, so fingers crossed, it may not look like this for

much longer. Centre for all National Express and other coach services.
National Express 08705 808080

■■ Rail

New Street Station (main station), Snow Hill, Moor Street
Adjoining the Pallasades shopping centre, New Street is the main place for commuters everywhere. Contact:
National Rail Enquiries 0345 48 49 50
Lost property ....(0121) 654 4286

■■ Tourist Information

Birmingham Convention and Visitor Bureaus
The NEC ....(0121) 780 4260
2 City Arcade ....(0121) 643 2514
ICC, Broad Street ....(0121) 665 6116
130 Colmore Road, Victoria Square
....(0121) 693 6300

■■ Taxis

Cabs, like most cities, are divided into three camps. There's the safe black cabs (T.O.A.), the varied private licensed cabbies, and the shonky, dangerous, but outright necessary unlicensed dodgy wide-boys who'll pretend they've left their license at home – the Corsa is the ideal car for a cab and no, they haven't been drinking. At night, the best places to catch them are down by the ramp at the Pallasades for the official queue for black cabs, Broad Street for hailing them down, and outside any dodgy club for a mixture of the lot (like Snobs for example).

■■ Central

BB's ....(0121) 693 3333
Blue Arrow ....(0121) 622 1000
Broadway Radio Cars ....(0121) 766 5661
Chequer Car Co......................(0121) 240 7777
Falcon Cars ....(0121) 454 5555
St Paul's Cars ....(0121) 233 0303
TOA..(0121) 427 8888

■■ Other Areas

Moseley
Ambassador Car ....(0121) 449 8888
Selly Oak/Harbourne
Quinborne Taxis ....(0121) 427 5000
Edgbaston
Yellow Cars ....(0121) 455 8888

www.itchybirmingham.co.uk

There's better things to spend money on.
Don't waste it on travel.

If you're under 26 or a student save £££'s on travel with a Young Persons' Discount Coachcard. Cards cost £9 and save you up to 30% off already low fares all year. Register online to receive special offers throughout the year.

For journey planning, tickets and coachcards
visit **GoByCoach.com** or call **08705 80 80 80**

NATIONAL EXPRESS

Check online for details.
Coach services depart from Digbeth Coach Station, Birmingham.

■■ Emergency Services

It's a big bad world out there and if you do get into a spot of bother you might need one of these numbers.

■■ Hospitals

Birmingham Childrens Hospital
Steelhouse Lane......................(0121) 333 9999

Birmingham Heartlands Hospital
Bordesley Green East ....(0121) 424 2000

City Hospital
Dudley Road ....(0121) 554 3801

Dental Hospital
St Chad's Queensway ....(0121) 236 8611

NHS Medical Centre at Boots
66 High Street ....(0121) 626 6000

University Hospital
Raddlebarn Road, Selly Oak (0121) 627 1627

■■ Police

For police stations in and around the city centre ....(0121) 626 5000
Police Central Lost Property Office
Digbeth Police Station, 113 Digbeth, Deritend ....(0121) 626 6000

■■ Rental Cars

Avis	(0121) 632 4361
Budget	(0121) 643 7743
Enterprise	(0121) 643 7743
Europcar	(0121) 622 5311
Hertz	(0121) 643 5387

■■ Universities

Aston switchboard	(0121) 359 6531
Aston Guild	(0121) 359 3611
B'ham switchboard	(0121) 414 3344
B'ham Guild	(0121) 472 1841
UCE switchboard	(0121) 331 5000
UCE Guild	(0121) 331 6801

itchy sms @
www.itchybirmingham.co.uk

www.itchy**birmingham**.co.uk

A
B
C
D
1
2
3
4
5
HARBORNE
LORDSWOOD ROAD
WENTWORTH ROAD
LONSDALE RD
RAVENHURST ROAD
PARK HILL
GORDON RD
STATION RD
HIGH STREET
SOMERSET RD
BARLOW'S RD
METCHLEY LANE
GREEN FIELD RD
HARBORNE PARK RD
WAR LANE
CONSTITUTION HILL
HAMPTON STREET
HOSPITAL STREET
NEW SUMMER ST
HENRIETTA STREET
LOWER LOVE
HANLEY
SHADWELL
LIVERY STREET
ST PAUL'S SQUARE
ST CHAD'S CIRCUS
POPE STREET
ALBION STREET
GRAHAM STREET
SUMMER HILL ROAD
KING EDWARD'S RD
GOODMAN ST
POWELL ST
CAMDEN STREET
GEORGE STREET
CHARLOTTE
NEWHALL STREET
LUDGATE HILL
WATER STREET
GREAT CHARLES ST QUEENSWAY
SNOW HILL STATION
SANDPITS
ST MARK'S CRESCENT
SUMMER ROW
FLEET STREET
LIONEL STREET
CHURCH STREET
BARWICK ST
COLMORE ROW
PIGEON PARK
CORNWALL
EDMUND STREET
EDWARD STREET
KING EDWARD'S RD
NIA
CAMBRIDGE STREET
PARADISE CIR
LIBRARY
PARADISE FORUM
CHAMBERLAIN SQUARE
VICTORIA SQUARE
WATERLOO STREET
CITY PLAZA
TEMPLE ST
NEEDLESS ALL
CANNON STREET
NEW STREET
PINFOLD STREET
STEPHENSON ST
TYNDALL ST
ICC
CENTENARY SQUARE
BROAD STREET
BRIDGE STREET
SUFFOLK ST QUEENSWAY
HILL STREET
NAVIGATION STREET
PALLASADES SHOPPING CEN
NEW STREET STATION
SHEEPCOTE STREET
BRINDLEY PLACE
GAS STREET
CARLTON TV
BERKLEY STREET
MORVILLE STREET
SHERBOURNE STREET
RYLAND STREET
GRANVILLE STREET
HOLLIDAY STREET
THE MAILBOX
SEVERN STREET
BLUCHER STREET
COMMERCIAL STREET
GOUGH STREET
UPR GOUGH ST
ELLIS STREET
MARSHAL ST
HINCKLEY ST
SMALLBROOK
THORP STREET
ESSEX
BROMSGROVE
BISHOPGATE STREET
TENNANT
BROADWAY PLAZA
FIVE WAYS
FIVE WAYS LEISURE
BATH ROW
IRVING STREET
TO HARBORNE
TO MOSELEY & SELLY OAK
EDGEBASTON SHOPPING CENTRE
P

E
F
G
H
NEW TOWN ROW
CORPORATION STREET
DARTMOUTH MIDDLEWAY
PARK ROAD
BAGOT STREET
STANIFORTH STREET
LOVE LANE
HOLT
LISTER STREET
PRINCIP STREET
PRICE STREET
ASTON UNI
ASTON TRIANGLE
WOODCOCK STREET
BRISTOL RD
HARROW ROAD
ALTON ROAD
BOURNBROOK RD
DAWLISH ROAD
TIVERTON ROAD
HUBERT ROAD
HEELEY ROAD
BRISTOL ROAD
EXETER ROAD
QUEENSWAY
CHILDREN'S HOSPITAL
JAMES WATT QUEENSWAY
STEELHOUSE LANE
NEWTON ST
JENNENS ROAD
BELMONT ROW
CARDIGAN STREET
GOPSAL STREET
SELLY OAK
MILLENNIUM POINT
GROSVENOR STREET
FOX STREET
CURZON STREET
EDWARD ROAD
GEORGE ST
TINDAL ST
MOSELEY ROAD
OAKFIELD RD
EDGBASTON RD
BANBURY STREET
BART ST
FAZELEY
DALE END
ALBERT
MARTINEAU PLACE
HIGH STREET
CARRS LANE
MOOR ST QUEENSWAY
MOOR ST STATION
PAVILION CENTRAL
NEW CANAL STREET
PICKFORD STREET
BARN STREET
RIVER STREET
PARK ROAD
LORNE RD
PARK HILL
CHANTRY ROAD
TRAFALGAR ROAD
NEW BULLRING
BULLRING
PARK STREET
ALLISON ST
MERIDEN STREET
FLOODGATE
EDGBASTON STREET
DIGBETH
DIGBETH COACH STATION
NATIONAL EXPRESS
MARKETS
ARCADIAN CENTRE
PERSHORE
SALISBURY ROAD
ALCESTER ROAD
OXFORD ROAD
SKINNER LA
BARFORD ST
MOSELEY
CRUMB-EYE DESIGN

index

Listing	Page No.	Grid Ref.
52 Degrees North	E518	/32
A2	D4	89
Academy, The	E4	68
Acid Test	D5	90
Ackers Trust	–	107
Actress & Bishop	C2	60
Adil's Balti	–	21
Airports	–	120
Alexandra Thtre	D5	101
All Bar One	B515	/36
Alton Towers	–	104
Angel's Café Bar	D6	80
Arca	E5	34
Artlounge, The	C5	97
Aston Villa F.C.	–	107
Autograph	D5	90
B'ham Academy	E4	106
B'ham Bullets	B4	107
B'ham City F.C.	–	107
B'ham H'drome	E6	101
B'ham Int. Casino	D2	109
B'ham Marriot	A6	118
B'ham Museum & Art Gallery	C4	102
B'ham Repertory Theatre	B5	102
B'ham Wheels Karting Centre	–	113
B3	D3	46
Bacchus	D4	46
Bakers	A6	68
Bank	B4	19
Bar 2 Sixty	B5	36
Bar Coast	E515	/34
Bar Med	E3	46
Bar Room Bar	E2	49
Barber Institute	–	102
Beauty Clinics	–	84
Belfry, The	–	113
Bell, The	B1	63
Bella Pasta	B4	25
Belmont Hotel	–	119
Bennetts	D415	/46
Berlioz	D4	91
BHS	D4	88
Bier Keller	D5	56
Bistro Lyonnaise	H6	20
Black Country Museum	–	104
Black Horse, The	F2	52
Bobby Browns	B5	70
Bonds	D2	70
Boots Bar	D5	80
Brannigan's	B5	36
Brasshouse	B5	53
Breed	H2	89
Briar Rose, The	D4	119
Bristol Pear, The	H2	61
Brook, The	H1	93
Brooklyn's Bar	A6	37
Bucklemaker Wine Bar & Restaurant	C2	51
Bull's Head	H5	65
Burlington Hotel	D4	118
Bus and local railways	–	120
Cadbury World	–	104
Café Lazeez	C5	21
Café Rouge	B5	20
Caffè Uno	D3	25
Campanile Hotel	–	119
Casa	B518	/37
Cathay	B6	12
Celebrity Balti	B5	21
Chamberlain Tower Hotel	B5	119
Chard House	–	119
China Court Restaurant		
Chung Ying	E6	13
Chung Ying Garden	E5	13
Circo	D5	46
City Plaza	D4	86
Cocks Moors Woods	–	113
Code	F5	70
Comfort Inn	D5	56
Copthorne Hotel	C4	119
Coventry City FC	–	108
Cross Bar, The	H6	51
Crown, The	D5	57
Crowne Plaza	C5	119
Cruise Flannels	D4	91
Cube	B5	38
Cult Clothing	D4	89
Dance Music Finder	D5	94
Dancefaze Records	–	94
Days Inn	C5	119
Denial	C5	18/50
Diesel	D4	89
Diwan	H4	22
DKNY	C5	91
DNA	D5	71
Drayton Manor Family Theme Park	–	105
DV8	E6	82
Eda	C5	91
Edwards	B5	38
Emergency no.s	–	123
Entertainment Centres	–	98
Expose Lap Dancing Club	4	110
Factorum & Firkin	D4	57
Fallow & Firkin	B1	63
Fiddle & Bone	B5	53
Figure of Eight	B5	58
Fire & Ice	D4	89
Fish	C5	30
Flares	D5	72
Fort, The	–	87
Fox, The	E6	82
Gap	D4	89
Gio's	C4	38
Glee Club, The	E6	107
Globe–Trotter	C5	97
Goose @ The Fighting Cocks	H5	65
Goose at the OVT	H2	61
Gosta Green	F2	53
Grand Prix Karting	–	113
Grandma Takes A Trip	E4	90
Green Man, The	C1	63
Green Room, The	D519	/34
Green Stadium	–	113
Greyhound Racing at Hall Green	–	
Greyhound Racing at Perry Barr Stadium	–	113
Grosvenor Casino	B5	10/100
Grosvenor Casino Bar	B5	39
GS3	D4	90
Gun Barrels, The	H2	62
Hairdressers	–	83
Harborne Golf Course	–	113
Harborne Stores, The	B1	63
Hard Rock Café	B5	39
Hard to Find Records	D5	94
Hatchford Brook	–	113
Health Clubs	–	84
Henry J Beans	B5	39
Hidden	E5	71
Hilltop	–	113
HMV	E4	94
Hogshead – Central	D3	57
Hogshead – Moseley	H5	65
Hollywood Bowl	–	101
Hospitals	–	123
Hush, The	D5	71
I am the King of Balti's		22
Ibis	E6	119
IceObar	D5	46
Ideal	E4	97
Ikon Gallery	A4	102
IMAX	F3	99
Indi	E622	/35
Indoor Market	E5	86
Ipanema	B5	10
Jay's	A6	23
Jam House, The	C2	60/72
James Brindley, The	B5	54
Jazz & Swing Record Centre, The	E2	94
Jester, The	D6	81
Jewel In The Crown	H5	23
Jewellery Quarter	C2	
Jibbering Records	H5	94
Jigsaw	D4	93
Jug of Ale	H4	66
K2	H5	23
Key Largo	B5	40
Khanum	H2	24
Kill For A Seat	F2	107
Kishimo Jin	D4	93
Las Iguanas	E6	11
Laters	–	116

126   itchy**birmingham** 2002

index

Le Petit Blanc	B4	20
Leftbank	B5	16
Legends Boardriders	D4	97
Legs 11	D5	110
Leisure Centres	–	85
Liberty's	–	73
Lickey Hills	–	105
Life	D4	90
Limeys	D4	90
Little Italy	H6	26
Livebait	B5	30
Love	D4	91
Maharaja	E6	24
Mailbox, The	D5	87
Majestic Snooker Club	D5	110
Malt House, The	B5	55
Marks & Spencer	E4	88
MC Man	D4	91
MC Woman	D4	93
McCluskys	D5	75
Medicine Bar	F5	48
Megabowl	E6	101
Mellow/Stoodies	B5	40
Merchant Stores	B5	40
Merry Hill Centre	–	87
MG's Pit Stop	E5	41
Midland Wheel Casino, The	–	110
Midlands Art Cntr	– 99/103	106
Missing	D6	80
Mongolian, The	C2	30
Moseley Dance Centre	H4	73
Muji	D4	89
Museum of the Jewellery Quarter	–	103
Mustard	–	74
Nando's	B5	11
National Paintball Fields	–	113
National Sealife Centre	B4	105
NEC Arena	– 103/106	
New Art Gallery, The	–	103
Newt & Cucumber	D4	57
NIA	B4	106
Nicholls Exclusive Clothing	D4	90
Nightingale, The	E6	82
Nostalgia & Comics	D5	93
Novotel	B5	119
O'Neill's	B5,E6 55/58/66
Oasis	D4	
Odeon Cinema	D4	99
Old Joint Stock	D4	58
Old Monk, The	B5	55
Old Orleans	B5	41
Original Levis Store	E4	91
Pallasades The	D4	87
Partner's Bar	D4	81
Patric Kavanagher	H5	66
Pavillion Central	E4	88
Pitcher and Piano	B5	42
Pizza Express	D4	26
Pizza Hut	E6	28
PJ's Moon & Sixpence	E6	58
Plough, The	B1	64
Poppy Red	E6	35
Premier Lodge	B5	119
Prince of Wales	H5	67
Priory Square Shopping Centre	E4	88
Que Club, The	F1	74
Quinn's	C5	50
Quo Vadis	E3	48
Quod	B5	28
Rackhams	E4	89
Rajdoot	E3	24
Reddington Rare Records F5	95
Reiss	D4	91
Rental Cars	–	123
Revolution	B5	42
Rhonit Zilkha	C5	93
Riley's	D6	110
Ronnie Scott's	B5 42/74/106
Ropewalk, The	C2	60
Royal Shakespeare		
Company	–	102
RSVP	E2	48
Sacks of Potatoes	F2	53
Saint Martins Market		
	E5	86
Saint Paul's	C2	17
Sam Wellers	D5	59
San Carlo Ristorante Pizzeria	D4	26
Sanctuary, The	F5	74
Santa Fe	C5	12
Sarah Priesler	–	97
Serene Order	D4	17
Shakespeare Houses, The		
	–	105
Shakespeare, The	D4	59
Shimla Pinks	B5	25
Shogun Teppan–Yaki		
	B5	29
Showcase Cinema	–	99
Simply Chinese	A4	14
Slug & Lettuce	D4	49
Snobs	C4	75
Snowhill Snooker Centre		
	D3	113
Sobar	E6 29/35
Spearmint Rhino's	A6	110
Spice Exchange	–	10
Sports Café	B5	42
Sportsman, The	C1	64
Square Peg	E2	59
Star City	–	101
Stonebridge Golf Centre		
	–	113
Stoodi Bakers	B5	75
Stuff & Co.	D4	97
Subway City	D2	82
Surfer's Paradise	B5	75
Swordfish Records	D4	95
Symphony Hall	B4 106
T.G.I. Fridays	–	10
Takeaways	–	114
Tamworth Snow Dome		
	–	107
Tap & Spile	B5	56
Tattoos & Piercing	–	84
Taxis	–	121
TCs	H2	62
Tempest Records	E3	95
Teppan Yaki	S5	29
Thai Edge	B5	31
Thai Mirage	E6	31
Tiger Tiger	A6 43/76
Tin Tins Cantonese		
	B5	14
Toad	D5	59
Tourist Info.	–	121
Tower Records	D4	95
Tower, The	–	76
Train stations	–	121
Trocadero, The	D4	59
UGC Cinema, Arcadian		
	E6	101
UGC Cinema Five Ways Leisure Park	A6	101
Universities	–	123
Varsity, The	B1	64
Village, The	H1	67
Virgin	E4	95
Walkabout	B5	43
Walsall	–	109
Warner Village Cinema		
	–	101
Waterhall Gallery	C4	104
Waterstone's	F2	93
West Bromwich Albion F.C.	–	109
West Midland Safari & Leisure Park	–	105
White Horse, The	B1	64
WHSmith	E4	93
WHSmith Travel	D5	94
Wine REPublic	C4 17/43
Wing Wah	–	14
Wolverhampton Wanderers F.C.	–	109
Works, The	D4	94
Xaymaca Exp.	–	12
XLs	A6	76
Yard of Ale	D4	60
Yo Yo	D4	90
Zanzibar	D5	76
Zig Zag	A6	110
Zizzi	C5	28

www.itchy**birmingham**.co.uk

THEY MUST PROMOTE YOU. YOU'VE GOT COMMITMENT.

BEWARE OF THE VOICES. FOR CAREER ADVICE WORTH LISTENING TO AND THOUSANDS OF JOBS, VISIT monster.co.uk